ISSUES
IN THE
TISSUES

Your Struggles Will Not Defeat Your Destiny

"LIVE"

MILLICENT ROBINSON

ISBN 978-1-0980-3479-5 (paperback)
ISBN 978-1-0980-3480-1 (digital)

Copyright © 2020 by Millicent Robinson

All rights reserved. No part of this publication may be reproduced, distributed, or transmitted in any form or by any means, including photocopying, recording, or other electronic or mechanical methods without the prior written permission of the publisher. For permission requests, solicit the publisher via the address below.

Christian Faith Publishing, Inc.
832 Park Avenue
Meadville, PA 16335
www.christianfaithpublishing.com

Printed in the United States of America

This book is dedicated to my handsome and loving husband Joshua Robinson, a great motivator in my life; my three children, Elysia Robinson, Lachane Robinson-Morris, and Shaquille Robinson, who are a great help and support to me in life and specifically with my writing.

Love you all!

CONTENTS

Preface 9
Chapter 1: Issues in the Tissues 15
Chapter 2: Press to Touch 22
Chapter 3: Touching Jesus Brings About Changes 29
Chapter 4: Victory Through Faith 36
Chapter 5: Maximize Your Courage 42
Chapter 6: Endure to Succeed 50
Chapter 7: Returning to a Situation is Not the Solution ... 58
Chapter 8: Controlling the Issues in the Tissues 65
Chapter 9: Spiritual Bankruptcy 71
Chapter 10: Faith Prevails Issues in the Tissues 79

The reviewer's acknowledgement:
Michelle Collins and Marcia Gardner my nieces & Bishop
E. R. Thomas, of Rest Tabernacle Church of Jesus Christ.

PREFACE

God always knows what is best for me.

I had no plans to become a writer, but God knew what was best for me. Despite being hindered by some physical hurdles, God said I will use you in spite of…

It was unfortunate that some time ago both my legs were injured, and I was unable to move around independently. As part of my recovery I had to visit the physiotherapist and chiropractor regularly. Every morning, I would bring a book with me to read to kill time while I waited. Funny enough one morning as I was waiting and reading, I heard a voice in my ear repeating, "Put the book down and start writing your own." I eventually responded to the voice which I determined was the leading of the Lord and said, "Yes, Lord I hear you, but what shall I write?"

When I got home from the doctor's appointment and told my daughter, Elysia, of my encounter, she was very excited and immediately began encouraging me to begin writing. Her exact words to me were "Go ahead, Mom!" Can't wait to see your first published book." The excitement in her voice motivated me and I began to write. At times, I didn't know if I was going or coming, but in spite of… God inspired me.

To God be the glory! He has allowed me to write and publish five books which include three children's books and two religious books.

God has done some awesome things in my life; I just didn't know how to share my story with the rest of the world. God gave me a vision of him sending me on a mission, ministering into the lives of people, but my answer was "How?". Although I was faced with "issues in my tissues" that were preventing me from even moving from my living room to the kitchen, God was telling me that there was an investment made in me that went beyond my pains. He revealed to me that the very things I believed were my setbacks was a set for my victory. However, in the midst of my pain, I couldn't understand the plan God had for my life.

I love God and I trust Him for all things, He is my Jehovah—Jireh (provider), my Jehovah—Rapha (healer); He heals all my diseases.

Just before my leg injuries I was also the victim of a heart attack. I waited twenty-one days for heart surgery in the ICU. At dawn on the twenty-second day, God gave me a dream. In the dream, he told me he "looked beyond my faults and saw my needs." I arose that morning feeling very relieved, excited and overwhelmed. I could hardly wait to be discharged because I knew I was healed. No sooner did the medical staff come in and after doing all their checks they advised me that my health condition changed, meaning that everything was back to normal and I could be moved to the "Step-Down Unit."

The cardiologist was very impressed with my recovery; however, he suggested that I not cancel the surgery due to other complications that might exist. I stood firm in my decision; I was healed. I told the doctor I didn't want to do a surgery anymore. God has healed me and what ever other complications need to be fixed in me God is able to fix it. By faith, I signed myself out of the hospital without surgery, medication or pain. God spontaneously healed me through his miraculous surgery—no scars or pain, Hallelujah, again faith has prevailed.

Just as the power of Jesus healed the woman with her issue of blood, I am a living testimony to the miracle working power of Jesus as I live a normal life. Thank you, God, for giving me a new heart.

Even with the leg injury and the heart attack it appears that those setbacks were not enough, shortly after my heart attack I was diagnosed with colon cancer. The prognosis from the doctor was that the disease was in my blood. He went through the lab test reports with me and my family, and then schedule an appointment to meet with a proctologist the next day. When I met with the proctologist, he educated me as well, explaining the nature and procedure of the surgery I would need to do and then asked me for my opinion. As crazy or dangerous as it sounds, I refused the surgery. The doctor responded to me "Well, it's your life I can't force you".

I knew this was a weapon being formed against me, but I took God at his word that it would not prosper. I thank God for my family and church family who pray earnestly for my healing. Through God's miraculous healing power, he did it again… I was healed.

A year later I had the follow-up test which came back negative. The doctors were astonished, and they said, "You are a woman of great faith". Despite my ongoing tests, I am confident that God didn't give me a breakthrough from the "issues in my tissues", he truly delivered me. You will hear more about the differences between deliverance versus breakthrough as you read, as they are not the same thing.

There is no way that I could end this without sharing the spirit of fear that had overwhelmed me at times when the situations appeared to be more than I could handle. When I was faced with hardships and major challenges, the do's and the don'ts, the why's and the what if's, and of course the but's, did I question God?, of course I did, I'd say "why me Lord?" and his answer was always the same "I've chosen you for this purpose". I had many sleepless nights and often tears would soak my pillow. Worrying had crippled my mind and thought processing to the point that I would sleep by my phone with the anticipation that something would go wrong. The scariest parts of my journey were the not knowing for certain if I would be around long enough to see my children grow up. While fear became a reality, God gave me a scripture; Psalms 118:17, "I shall not die but live and declare the works of the Lord". This became my literal reality. You will not succumb to the issues in your tissues, "Live!"

Readers of this book, please read with confidence. We were all born with issues in our tissues; we all have different experiences and different diagnosis. Going through painful processes can cause emotional stress, psychological stress, spiritual stress, mental stress, and physical stress. All that you have been through or are still going through is an encouragement to others. "Many are the afflictions of the righteous, but the Lord delivered him out of them all" (Psalm 34: 19). You will not succumb to the issues in your tissues. "Live!"

This book reflects on a certain woman in the Bible with an issue of blood.

> St. Luke 8: 43–48 (KJV)
> "And a Woman having an issue of blood twelve years, which had spent all her living upon physicians, neither could be healed of any, came behind him and touched the border of his garment: and immediately her issues of blood stanched.

And Jesus said, "Who touched me?" When all denied, Peter and they that were with him said, "Master, the multitude throng thee and press thee, and sayest thou, who touched me?" And Jesus said "Somebody hath touched me: for I perceive that virtue is gone out of me."

And when the woman saw that she was not hiding, she came trembling and falling down before him, she declared unto him before all the people for what cause she had touched him and how she was healed immediately.

And Jesus said unto her, "Daughter, be of good comfort: thy faith hath made thee whole; go in peace."

CHAPTER 1
Issues in the Tissues

The Bible speaks of a certain woman, a woman of no identity. "Certain" is not a name or by any means an identification. To add to understanding of who this woman was; this woman while undervalued by society because of her circumstances, was no stranger to God: he knew her very well.

> "Thine eyes did see my substance, yet being unperfect, and in thine book, all my members were written which in continuance were fashioned. When as yet there was none of them. How precious also are thy thoughts unto me, O God! How great is the sum of them?" (Psalm 139: 16–17).

God knew about this woman's issues and yet still had a plan for her life. A plan she could not have dreamt of, a plan that went beyond her issues. God has a way of showing up when you least expect it. He may not work on your plans and in your timing, but God works on time. He is aware of all your special needs. He will not cancel you out because you are his priority. God is positioning you for his season; to work on you in your season. This is your breaking point. Sometimes God takes you to a breaking point to test your level of faith and obedience. He breaks you and fashions you to make you ready for his potential use so that his name will be glorified. This is your time to tell the devil "enough is enough." Even when you aren't sure where your next meal is coming from, be sure of your season. I believe the woman was unsure of her next coin. The Bible said she had spent all her money on the physicians and accomplished nothing. However, when she recognized her season was "now", that her healer, her redeemer, her Jesus was near; she stepped out of her impossibilities into possibility.

God will not confuse your mind with scheduled appointments, only to have them canceled and re-scheduled, but in your time of despair when no one seems to care, Jesus will appear to show you that he does care.

With the love of God there is absolutely no place for isolation and separation to oppress or depress you, but rather to motivate, empower, and to assure you that you are a part of society and under no circumstances should you feel yourself lower in any rank. There are always opportunities, but sometimes the problem is underestimating God's abilities. You are always telling yourself you are not good enough, you are not qualified, you don't have what it takes to make it to the next level. Be encouraged and take the challenge, you can make it if you try. Do not let your setback be because of you.

Being isolated and separated from society is not a healthy environment that anyone wishes to encounter or live in. Is there anyone who can predict their future? No one can; only God knows what is ahead. The hymnology said, "Many things about tomorrow I don't seem to understand but I know who holds tomorrow and I know who holds my hand."

"The Woman's" issues were not contagious and there was no need for her to be quarantined; but it was necessary, for God was positioning freedom from cultural ritual to grace and mercy. Thank you, Almighty God for truth and grace through our Lord and Savior Jesus Christ, who shed his blood on the Cross of Calvary for the sins of humanity. God has a set plan for your life you can only wait for God's plan to materialize, he will not alter or change what he has designated for your life, but he will comfort you with his word.

God's words of comfort make all the difference when you are going through your moments; pains so excruciating pressing against your sciatic nerve, that stabbing pain in the head or in other parts of your body that are so overwhelming that even pain killers don't help. The good old home remedies you thought would have kicked in and bring results fail to bring relief, never mind the lingering pains that disturb your sleep in the midnight hour, when nothing helps it would seem as if the clock is stuck to the hands; seconds feel like hours and everything seems unreal. You tell yourself it must be your imagination and with the fear of your pain you are constantly hoping for morning to appear, but the hours are just not moving fast enough. God, where are you? I need you, God! In those lonely hours, those grievous lonely hours, that gentle voice appears bringing you comfort and cheers saying "Dry your tears, I am your Balm in Gilead and I can heal your body and ease your pains. I am your refuge and strength a very present help in trouble. Be not afraid though the earth is removed and though the mountains are carried into the sea. Be still and know that I am God." Leave it up to God. He can fix it if you allow him to. Let him deal with your situation because God knows exactly what to do.

Financial impingement was not a concern at the offset of her issues; her focus was on her physician and her health issues. Did you know that money has power? Yes, it does. It is the answer to many things except Salvation. For those who treasure materialistic gains, money can bring you into high places, it gives you the ability to do things, get things independently, and bring influence and impact over the life of others who are less fortunate. It can gain you respect, especially when you know how to invest. But that same power that money brings can also be used to break you. It can bring you down and embarrass you. Here is some advice: never let your money control you. You should be the controller over your money not the other way around. Money can be a big issue when there is not enough to spend, never mind when there is none, for rent, mortgage, bus tickets, a bag of milk or for the next meal. In that stressful moment of your financial embarrassment, you can only seek for favors form your Jehovah Jireh, your father the great Creator, the supplier of all your needs. The only requirement includes the following actions: knock, ask, and seek. There are also the money robbers who carefully plan how to rob others, sometimes by violence. Does this sound crazy? As crazy as it may sound its the reality; these are issues in the tissues. You will read more about money power in the next chapters.

I can't imagine this woman's visits to the physicians. Was she transported to the physician, or was it an in-house visit? Since she was considered unclean to be in public places according to the cultural ritual, this woman was like a prisoner in her own house, but well disciplined.

She was tragically confined to her house; she could not be seen in public places, not even the marketplace. This was quite tragic for a person to be in such a position of "house imprisonment" for twelve years. Making matters worse, her health issue was not getting better but rather deteriorating and her money now became an issue. The Bible said, "she had suffered many things of many physicians" (St. Luke 8:43). My assumption is that there were other issues plaguing her tissues, and of course this would have to be an opportunity to affect the mind as she struggled with such chaotic experiences in her life.

There were opportunities for other issues and their occurrences to invade her tissues such as frustration, emotional, psychological, physical, and spiritual stress but she did not allow any of these things to get the best of her. She got the gut feeling that great change was coming her way and it was only a matter of time for it to be fulfilled.

Do not let your emotions get the best of you, no matter how chaotic life gets, you are already an overcomer just believe in yourself. Know how powerful you are and listen to the voice of Jesus. He is trying to communicate with you just as he was speaking to the woman with the issue. He is calling you from sickness to health, from poverty to wealth, from doom to destiny, from failure to purpose, from sin to grace, and from a life of limitations to a life without borders. The enemy has targeted you to distract you, but don't get distracted, keep your focus, He will not have the upper hand of you, and neither will you be embarrassed by that mind abuser, our adversary—the devil. Use the Word of God as your weapon and armor to cover your mind. Let the impostor know that Jesus died for you that you might inherit eternal life in abundance, your unlimited luxury. There are times when you may feel despondent because of the messiness of life, but there is still hope. Look for your light at the end of your tunnel; the light of hope.

That light is Jesus, taking you out of your dark spots, your misery, your fear, and your issues. God is getting you ready for your next level. You do not easily get recognized when you're down in your lowest valley, but that's okay; not everyone gets noticed when they are undergoing training. This could be that you are not yet qualified for that significant job opportunity, but if success in your dreams, nothing will be able to stop you. In your gloom and despair, God will furnish you with peace, lead you into green pastures, and refresh you with his cool, cool waters from the overflowing streams, the rivers of life. Unnoticed does not mean you're forgotten (Psalm 23).

The unknown woman with her issues was unnoticed but not forgotten; her valley experience was necessary. Valley experiences are necessary for all believers. Your God is creative; he's making the best of you when you are in the valley. The valley is the best place to fast and pray. It is there that God gives you visions and revelations because you are alone with God, free from the outside world. What better place would you wish to be? Just you and your God, on a one-on-one.

It was God's decision to take you to the valley, preparing you for his finished product, the best that he wants you to be. God's preservation will enable you to stand throughout the hard times, as you encounter testing, trials, tribulations, and frustrations. These are a part of your package as you navigate life; be sure to know that there is a purpose for your journey. There are opportunities available. God saw potential in you, the job description is amazing, and you have the skills, but you need training to get to the next level. God will place you in the valley training you to be his mouthpiece, he knows your destiny, but also sees the fear in you. Jesus saw potential in Peter, but he also knew that Peter was not able to stand up well under pressure. The evidence of this is when Peter denied that he knew Jesus, because of fear for his own life; he said, "I knew not the man" (Matthew 26:72). You may go through your circumstances and may even go as far as denying the Christ and think that all hopes are gone. "O wretched man that I am," said Paul (Romans 7:24-25).

God desires to build you and use you. Will you let him? You are the right person for the position; what a blessing to be known as such.

Jesus took Peter to his valley of decision. He was pressured, when Jesus questioned him a few times, "Peter, do you love me more than these?" Peter responded, "Yes Lord you know I love thee", Jesus said, "feed my sheep" (St. John 21:15-17). Jesus was ready to use Peter, but he had some issues that needed to be dealt with; the issue of fear was confronting him. Peter saw Jesus' suffering and he was ready to make that move to walk in Jesus' footsteps. He was being empowered to take up the mantel and do Gods works; there was leadership in him. Jesus knew Peter was capable of the tasks ahead. Peter had all the necessary skills to lead. Jesus said, "Thou art Peter, and upon this rock I will build my church; and the gates of hell shall not prevail against it" (Matthew 16:18). If there are issues sticking out in your mind, destroying your spiritual growth, it is like a disease living in the tissues, breaking down the immune system and making it harder for your tissues to survive. Fear is hindering and will keep pressing against your will trying to win; God is able to break that cycle.

You may go as far as denying the Christ, and even think all hope is gone, or even question your purpose being here. God is willing to give hope to the hopeless, life to the lifeless and faith to the faithless. Never take matters in your own hands, there is no point in giving up because God is no stranger to what you are experiencing. He alone can walk you through your destiny, believe in your God and let him be your first and last resort. Mrs. E.E. Williams said it well, "I have made my choice forever, to walk with Christ the Lord, not from my soul can saver, while I am trusting in his word. I the lowly path has taken, rough and tiresome though it is, although despise forsaken Jesus, I go through with thee".

The woman with her issue of blood was able to stand under pressure. She never complained in her situation but exercised her faith and patience because she knew her moment was coming when she would be released out of her valley, and find her victory. Her pre-existing condition would be no more a plague in her life.

There is a point and time in your life when you must come to a decision. The decision, that enough is enough! After all I have been though, enough is enough! This was possibly what was going through this woman's mind. The doctors took all her life savings and were unable to cure her diseases; now her issues got worse but in God she put her trust.

Reviewing her status, this certain woman, a Jew, had an issue of blood for twelve years. She was isolated, and what little money she had all went towards her medical bills. Worst of all after all of that she still was not cured of her illness. But whatever she was going through, it was not God's will to have her die. It was a setup for God's glory to be revealed. Jesus was proving her equality, and above equality he was saying, "I don't need your money, I don't need your riches, your silver or gold. All I need is your mind. You belong to me. I made you, body, soul and spirit. There is absolutely no charge for your healing."

After you have suffered many things, even when you can't understand, just believe that God is processing you for a brighter future. You will not succumb to your prolonged complications and the risky situations. Your great, omnipotent God is only a touch away. Press to touch.

CHAPTER 2
Press to Touch

The woman pressed to touch. Here Jesus had no tolerance for intolerance. Jesus was surrounded by a great multitude; some took offense at his teaching and his miracles, especially if he healed on the Sabbath day. In other words, there were scrutinizers, criticizers, and faultfinders among the crowd, ready to judge or condemn. Optimistically, Jesus had a job to get done, he was unstoppable, and nothing could have prevented him. He has all authority and power and had no tolerance for intolerance. He is the God of special needs and heals the people of special needs. "Ye that is whole need, not a physician" (Luke 5:31).

Jesus was confronted with two patients with special needs: an obscure woman with very critical needs for twelve years and a twelve-year-old girl who was terminally ill. Realistically, you would think the young girl would be the greater priority because her father was a famous ruler, and she was at the point of death. She was also young and innocent, with an expected future ahead.

Jesus, who has power over all things, came to make an amendment to the rituals. Jesus made the woman the greater on his list of priorities. Amazingly, Jesus was making a difference here between the known and the unknown. Jairus already had a name and fame; he was a ruler of the synagogue whose one and only daughter was critically ill. Life was at stake; imaginarily, the people thought that Jesus would have to be subordinated to Jairus's request being as he was a ruler of the synagogue. The unclean woman was of a low degree. Again, the ritual was that the Jewish men should protect themselves by carefully avoiding touching, speaking to, or even looking at women in her condition. In Jesus's mind, this suffering woman, should not by any means be overlooked, as God's creation, attention, and respect were necessary at any cost.

When visiting an emergency room, it doesn't matter what time you arrived. When another patient comes in with greater issues, they immediately become the greater priority. My issues were a priority. My aching heart and bleeding eyes pressed to touch Jesus. I needed a heart surgery and a possible blood transfusion, I was weak and death was lurking at my door, I was lonely in my hospital bed but I lifted my faith and touched Jesus and that heart attacked dried up just like the issue of blood.

You may have or are currently experiencing issues of which you have been praying to God about for a long time. It might seem like you have been forgotten or that God will not answer you. It may be that you are experiencing a job crisis, financial demands, struggling to put your children through college/university, finding that sanctified wife, getting that godly husband, that car, that house, to be spiritual elevated or motivated, to have complete healing from all your diseases, or to remove the spirits of rebelliousness from your child/children's lives. You may also be praying for your children to leave that bad company that is influencing them, blocking them from aspiring to the call of God upon their lives. Just hold out a little while longer, you are on God's priority list; God will not bump you off his list. Just be patient and keep your focus. There is no need to get restless or even to complain. Keep your mind intact, don't be pre-occupied lest your name should called, and you are not in the present to hear your name. What is the point of waiting for such a long time and missing your purpose?

God has a set appointment for you, and you do not want to miss that. Stay in the room, stay in God's presence, remain in his plan. If you leave the room now you might not have time to return. If you take the risk, you might end up in experiencing setbacks. The wait is necessary and you as a candidate must have patience, you must know how to wait. The KJV of Isaiah 40: 28–31 says

> "Hast thou not known? Hast thou not heard, that the everlasting God, the LORD, the Creator of the ends of the earth, fainteth, neither is weary? There is no searching of his understanding. He giveth power to the faint; and to them that have no might he increaseth strength. Even the youths shall faint and be weary, and the young men shall utterly fall: But they that wait upon the LORD shall renew their strength; they shall mount up with wings as eagles; they shall run, and not be weary, and they shall walk, and faint."

God can teach you how to wait if you rely on him. The wait is necessary, and nothing will go wrong no matter how the situation appears to you. You will not succumb to your issues; even though tissues get infirmed, trust your God. He will lead you through all this. Giving up is not an option. Suicide is not an option. The word of God is your strength and comfort. God's words will reach every wound. His blood is the antibiotic and the antidote for every wound. The word of God penetrates the hearts. Hebrews 4: 12 says "For the word of God is quick, and powerful, and shaper than any two-edged sword, piercing even to the dividing asunder of soul and spirit, and of the joints and marrow, and is a discerner of the thoughts and the intents of the heart". God sees your pain and sees your struggles. Even if your issues are obscure, God knows about it, you shall live and not die.

God already knows about your crises. Others only assume or ask to consume with bad intentions. Some will even go as far as digging up your past. That is what condemners do; they seek ways to bury your potentials and devour your God-given talents. "For God has not given us the spirit of fear, but of power and of love and of a sound mind" (2 Timothy 1:7).

ISSUES IN THE TISSUES

You should never be a quitter, but a fighter and a survivor. You must have that determination to keep your focus to finish God's task. He laid hands on you because he saw hope, purpose, and courage in you. You are tough enough, you are powerful, you are chosen, and God has a great plan for your life. Issues will never make you lose your mind because you know yourself, and you know your God. You know the connection you feel from Jesus holding your hands, who he is to you, and what he requires of you. You have got to be special to be on God's priority list; you are in God's spotlight and you don't even realize it. Defeat will not have the upper hand over you. It doesn't matter how bad the issues get, Jesus's blood becomes the cleanser, shield, shelter, protector and coverage over your mind. The enemy will not dictate any negativity over your mind. You are God's blood washed; he will take care of your issues.

A woman that was completely undervalued, unnamed, unannounced, outcasted, and isolated, was now to be treated like a person, not as someone who suffered from the disease of leprosy.

Let us look back at Jairus. He was a ruler of the synagogue and I believe that he was well known by most of the people in the crowd and had been noticed by many. His job was at risk but at that time the greater priority was his daughter's life, which had superseded his job. While many of the Jews were against Jesus, Jairus was not looking at his prestigious career, he was concerned about life. If the people had decided to stone Jairus for intermingling, peradventure he would not even care, all he wanted was for his daughter to live.

I believe there was a connection in the Holy Ghost, from Jesus Christ to the woman that caused her to get out of her place of confinement to be in the crowd. Indeed, "Jesus was passing her way" that day. Jesus is in control and can be in touch with the feelings of our infirmities. One would think she would have been weak after her prolonged bleeding, but whatever the case, weakness was no more a factor. She had only one aim and desire going through her mind, which was to press through the crowd to touch Jesus; she "pushed" to touch.

Whatever you may be experiencing in your life, whether it be anxiety, or overwhelming issues that make you somewhat uncomfortable or feel alienated. It may be that you can't find the spirit of forgiveness or that you're dealing with in-depth hurt and pain that others can't see, but only you and your Creator. Internalizing pain is very dangerous; it is a silent killer that brings about stress that oppresses your tissues. It plagues and depresses your mind.

Despite inward pain, anger that will not go away and issues that you feel are too personal to disclose or discuss, I want to remind you that there is a friend that is closer than any other friend, a friend of the friendless, a friend when others failed, a friend you can go to in prayer. Press to touch Jesus, tell him of your issues one on one. You have a savior who loves you and will never leave you. John 15: 13 says, "Greater love hath no man than this, that a man lay down his life for his friends".

It is now time to get out of your secret places, those places of confinement; there is no need to isolate yourself anymore. Jeremiah thought that God had forgotten him, but he found himself in a place where he pressed to touch God for his recovery. Lamentations 3:1-4 says, "I am a man that hath seen affliction by the rod of his wrath. He hath led me, and brought me into darkness, but not into light. My flesh and my skin hath he made old; he hath broken my bones". These verses stood out to me because amidst all his experiences, in his valley he found consolation as he touched God. Verses 18–24 of Lamentations continues, "And I said, my strength and my hope perishes from the LORD: Remembering mine affliction and my misery, the wormwood, and the gall. My soul hath them still in remembrance and is humbled in me. This I recall to my mind, therefore have, I hope. It is of the Lord's mercies that we are not consumed because his compassions fail not. They are new every morning: great is thy faithfulness. The LORD is my portion, saith my soul; therefore, will I have hope."

The negative issues you struggle with are only a set up to set you back. There are things you will have to ignore in order to go forward. There are some things that do not make sense and you will have to let go of because if you hold unto them, you defeat your purpose in God. You are too smart to allow the unwelcome element to reside in your territory. Crises might come but shall not reside for Jesus' blood stain has already taken up residence and will block every negative thought that approaches your mind.

You are fully equipped with all the necessary tools to maintain your godly character. Despite all the recurring setbacks, you are intelligent, and you know your surroundings. When you are under attack, be sure to be fully armed with the Word of God which is your shield. God already empowered you for this task; there is no need to be in doubt, for the battle is going to be in your favor. Fight courageously and wisely to withstand evil. If you have already deemed yourself a winner…aren't you? You will not surrender at any cost; God gave you integrity and power and has placed you in a leveraging position to accomplish his purposes while you are overcoming oppositions. Your outcome will be greater as God uses you.

You are aware of the fact that your opposer will present himself unaware, telling you things to mess-up your mind, telling you things like "You won't make it", "You're too messed-up to pray", or "Why don't you take a break?" thereby having you on his roller coaster. The adversary did that to Jesus when he took him up on a pinnacle to be tempted by him. The devil himself is messed up and seeking ways to mess up others. When the devil comes knocking at your door, turn up the heat by praying more, fast more, and worship God more. Just give God more of you. You know what prayer has done for you in the past and what prayer is doing for you right now. Your future is based on prayer; prayer opens the doors to success, victory, and empowerment. It is a way to communicate with God. Prayer closes every door of satanic powers and pulls down strongholds, defeating the purposes of the enemy. The devil is a thief with tongue of butter, packed with genericity and possessing nothing. He will tell you things such as "Church is not the place for you", or "It is too boring", while at the same time he's trying to pull you into his domain, pulling you like a spider pulling a fly into its web. You are not a fly, God purposed you and appointed you for greatness. He has appointed you from your mother's womb and God is getting you ready for an assignment your opponent is aware of. You shall not by any means be blindfolded by this craftiness. He thought he could have stressed out Jeremiah with issues of the people in Jerusalem, but God was getting Jerimiah ready for a greater task. God would depend on him to speak to his people, Israel. God first humbled him then used him exclusively to bring out his plan. God will use you if you avail yourself to him. God used Jeremiah despite the many complexities; the issues that plague his tissues. He said, "Remembering mine affliction and my misery, the wormwood, and the gall. My soul hath them still in remembrance and is humbled in me. This I recall to my mind, therefore have, I hope. It is of the Lord's mercies that we are not consumed because his compassions fail not. They are new every morning: great is thy faithfulness. The LORD is my portion, saith my soul; therefore, will I hope in him" (Lamentation 3:19-24).

When God is ready for you to move, he will make your situation uncomfortable; it is his way of getting you ready for the next level.

God's thoughts towards mankind is so amazing. More specifically, the love and immense care he has towards this whole creation. You don't have to be introduced to him by anyone for him to love you. You do not have to be special to be loved by him; you don't have to be wealthy for him to be in your life. You don't have to be special for God to use you, but he uses you because he specialized in you. You don't have to be extraordinary to impress God for him to see you, you only have to humble yourself and he will exalt you. Your God is the super-extraordinary God; Omnipotent and incredible. We are grateful for the communication and access we have with and to our Creator. We do not have to go through rituals, we only have to press to touch and he will hear us when we call.

Bear in mind all that you are experiencing now, is definitely a set-up plan to set you back. However, the Almighty God already set you on high; he sees that the desire of your opponents is to mince you into pieces, but God has your back. His strength and courage will uphold you that you faint not. He has chosen you for this test because he knew you have trusted him. God wants you to position yourself and move beyond your fear with confidence that your Creator is in control.

Press to touch, you shall not die but live.

CHAPTER 3
Touching Jesus Brings About Changes

Touching Jesus brings about changes. The unnamed woman approached the crowd with an attitude. She pressed with confidence and as she pressed, she stretched forth her hand, and grabbed Jesus's garment. Immediately, her faith transcended and was met with the healing power of Jesus; instantaneously her world was completely changed. Touching Jesus brought divine healing; her bleeding issue stopped and hence came her deliverance. She was now able to meet in all public places and to do all things conveniently.

One touch affected her body immediately; the transaction of her faith and the power that left Jesus was instant. Her change came so spontaneously she was overwhelmed and filled with such amazement. Not only was she healed, but she realized that her issue was not hidden amongst the crowd and neither was the purpose of touching Jesus.

It is important to note, Jesus did not ask her to testify to the crowd of her healing, but there was an internalized overflowing joy which was very hard to resist. She could only release her joy in the atmosphere; the glorious change that Jesus has brought to her life; so, her testimonial went viral. Bill Gaither penned these words, "He touched me, Oh He touched me, and oh the joy that floods my soul! Something happened and now I know, He touched me and made me whole." The woman was overjoyed to be healed by one touch.

I also experienced the effects of one touch that healed my tissues. The doctors were amazed the next morning of the healing virtue and restoration to my tissues. Hope of living rejuvenated my system; I could not touch my heart but the dented heart I saw before on the monitor is now healed and looked normal again. I too, was overjoyed.

When Jesus changes you, delivers you and heals you, you should not feel embarrassed, let others know what Jesus has done for you. Be excited. Reach out to others; it is possible they too can be healed through your testimony. That broken heart can be mended, and souls can be touched. Your testimony can assure others that Jesus can do the same for them, and even more. God doesn't deliver us for us to keep it to ourselves, but to impart to others that they too can be delivered; with him there is no limitation or segregation. The woman was nervous. She came trembling, but she did not allow herself to be consumed by those issues; she only wanted to touch Jesus.

The hands transfer and receive; it is the activity of the whole arm which collects messages, exporting and importing information. Hands give blessing, they are expressive and can be used as an awesome tool. In general, it is strength, power and protection. They give hospitality and stability. We often use the phrase "gives a lending hand" to show the significance. It is not clear whether it was her right hand or left hand that she used, but it would not have made a difference, she only wanted to touch Jesus. As believers, we raise our right hand in worship because we know that our God is seated at the right hand of power.

We frequently pray and ask Jesus to hold us with his wounded hands because as believers we know that Jesus's wounded hands bring healing and deliverance. We believe through the power of Jesus's hands touching us, we are healed.

I have received healing by Jesus touching me many times and by faith, believing I have been made whole. I am also sure he has done the very same for you.

The unknown woman broke the rule that held her hostage as an unclean person approaching Jesus. Consequently, it was also inappropriate for a Jewish man, practically a rabbi, to touch a female, but Jesus flipped the coin as I made mentioned in previous chapters. This was a way to let the Jews know that Jesus came to break the cycle, to remove segregation and to show equality. The Jews lived by the letter, (the law), everything must be followed closely and kept unbroken. Thanks be to our Lord and Savior Jesus Christ who "came not to destroy the law but to fulfill" (Matthew 5:17 KJV) the law. Jesus Christ gave his life for our sins when he died on Calvary for humanity to be free from such rituals.

God has granted such privilege, freedom, change, and equality. We can now cry Abba Father today. We can touch Jesus at any given time, in any place. It is indeed a privilege that should not be taken lightly. You have the right to call on Jesus. He is your daddy, your caretaker, life-giver, and sustainer; you live today because Christ lives.

This was an awesome change in this woman's life. Her future, her dispassion, demeanor, and her charisma were changed. What great tenacity she used, that Jesus could have felt that special touch. Amazingly and miraculously, egalitarianism (equal right) was given to her. He called her "daughter". "Daughter thy faith hath made thee whole, go in peace" (Luke 8:48).

When God changed you and gave you a second chance, there is absolutely no time for setbacks. He purposed you to set you on high; he made things happen to you, to get the best of you. Immediately this woman's life was changed because of her faith that was now invested in Jesus Christ. Her gain and long-term goal was healing. This phenomenal investment had a great impact universally; it has impacted me, and without a doubt you and others.

What influenced me most and allowed me to be gracefully involved in this woman's life story was her actual faith; she put her faith into action. James 2:26 (NKJV) says "For as the body without the spirit is dead, so faith without works is dead also".

The great significance about this woman was that she should not have been seen in public places. Her isolation and quarantine disposition brought great fear upon her. Faith is the substance of things hoped for, the substance of her faith allowed Jesus to be connected to her. I imagine it was like electricity coursing through her as she touched Jesus without hesitation or resistance. For the job to be accomplished, faith must meet faith. When faith gets in action, works are done. To God be the glory, with him all things are made possible.

Fear can be a monster in a person's life, festering in the mind with creepy imaginary thoughts importing and exporting negativities. Negative thoughts will bring you to a state of isolation, separation from society, and away from those who love you. The devil is trying to build a wedge between you and your maker, but just encourage yourself because God is changing you and the devil doesn't like it. When he had you, he used you for his convenience or as his agent. He is coming after you with full force, trying to bring back your past. He wants you to feel guilty of the past, feel so condemned that you can't even pray. Roman 8: 1(KJV) says, "There is therefore now no condemnation to them which are in Christ Jesus, who walk not after the flesh but after Spirit".

The devil is an absolute liar, despicable and deceptive. All his thoughts are evil because he's evil; he will not tell you to study God's words, to pray, or to fast because these are massive weapons against him. If you want to have him on the run, just get on your knees and use the blood of Jesus against him at all his approaches. There is power in the name of Jesus.

The devil possesses stubborn will. He takes rejection as an invitation, or as an opportunity to find other ways to tempt you. Luke 4:13 (NIV) says, "When the devil had finished tempting Jesus, he left him until the next opportunity came". The blood of Jesus does work; it worked all the time for me and will do the same for you.

One day on my way to church I was attacked by a gunman, and the only defense I had was the blood of Jesus. I shot the gunman three times with the blood of Jesus, and the gunman ran. This experience proves that the blood brings changes and is your defense when you are in trouble. If you want the atmosphere around you to change, just reach out to the blood of Jesus.

He will tempt you to read dirty magazines, watch dirty movies, go to the club, become addicted to drugs or alcohol, to abuse your spouse, your children, family, or friends. I sincerely believe you will not be abused or misused by the devil's tricks. Jesus has armed you, as he did with David; he turned your life around when he touched you.

ISSUES IN THE TISSUES

You are godly, you are a child of God and you are a Christian. Let Satan know you are aware of his unhealthy lifestyle and that his payout is death. You are walking Christ-like because God favored you.

Jesus's touch causes change, change brings favor, favor brings love, love brings passion, passion brings pain, pain brings agony, agony brings death, death brings life, and life brings hope, hope that makes us not ashamed. Christ died that we might have life more abundantly. There is no need to settle for less when your Creator means the world to you.

Disappointments will not have you broken. You may be down for a moment, but you will eventually realize that the disappointment worked out for your good. God has some good stuff lined up for you. There are great opportunities behind your disappointment. Always look at the bigger picture and don't forget the great things God has already done in your life. He will never change. Always think the best is yet to come and keep your mind open; give room for changes, and opportunities.

God promoted Joshua to leadership because God saw the potential in him. Joshua already knew the ways of the children of Israel, that they were set in their ways and not up to change. Joshua had to be committed to God's command, for better or for worst; Joshua had to be committed to the task because change had to come through him. God desired the children of Israel to change their ways so that they could have a better inheritance. It is often hard to introduce change when there is no tolerance for change. Change is important, it is like a medicine to the mind. The changes that we accept in our lives should be positive. Whether these are lifestyle, environmental or spiritual changes, they must be in support of leading you closer to the will of God. Therefore, God encourages Joshua, "Be strong and courageous" (Joshua 1: 6-7). You are strong and filled with purpose. A powerful worrier is what God has made you to be. Do not accept the spirit of inferiority or inadequacy. You have the power and you have the anointing of the Holy Ghost upon your life.

"Behold, I give unto you power to tread on
serpents and scorpions, and over all the power of

the enemy: and nothing shall by any means hurt you" (Luke 10:19).

God's word is powerful. He has never lost a battle and He always win. The Bible states that God loves the world so much that he gave his only son "that whosoever believeth in Him should not perish but have everlasting life" (John 3:16).

You might be going through an unexplainable situation, which is no doubt a problematic issue that might be getting worse; sometimes things get worse before they can get better. All the things you are exposed to that cause panic are deteriorating your tissues and destroying your mind. Let go of the things that are holding you hostage, the disease that is plaguing you and anything that is bombarding your friendship and overall relationship. They have no long-term benefits. Therefore, it makes no sense holding on to them; they will do more harm than good.

You have the ability to recap, retract, and navigate your way to change. Change is personal and begins inside you. Often, we look at others to first make the change, and if they don't, we won't. Change is not about competing against another, but rather recognizing the things that need to be adjusted in your life. On the other hand, change can be rewarding as it can brings impact to a community, and to people who are less fortunate. Change can bring deliverance universally like the unknown woman with her faith.

Reach out and touch Jesus by faith to expect a change. Come with the expectation that each issue will be removed. If you feel that you're falling, don't give up; you can get back up again. If you have not spoken to your issues, it is about time you start. Start speaking to your issues, call them out by name and delete them out of your system. Call to that cancer, that chest pain, arthritis, asthma, diabetes, high blood pressure, heart attacks, aches and pains of all sorts. Decree and declare in the name of Jesus, elevate your faith for deliverance is a touch away. Put your faith into action and press to touch Jesus. Touching Jesus will bring about changes. Poverty and financial barriers must go in Jesus's name. Speak God's promises over your life: "The Lord is my Shephard I shall not want he maketh me to lie down in green pastures" (Psalm 23:1). "The earth is the Lord and the fullness thereof the world and they that dwell therein" (Psalm 24:1).

The unnamed woman came to a final decision; she chose life and compassion over self-pity. Self-pity was poison to her structure, but her faith superseded all her barriers. Absolutely no ritual could have prevented her from receiving her miraculous touch; she pressed to touch Jesus. Touching Jesus brought about change, and her change came by faith.

CHAPTER 4
Victory Through Faith

To receive my victory, I had to maintain my focus. The center of my interest was to be healed, and the activity of my mind was to move by faith. With this, I maintained a positive outlook. A positive focus means having the control over your mind, feelings, and your emotion. The things you put in your mind represent you, and you are what your mind represent. Whoever you think you are will play out on its own, but whatever you speak over your life can change the trajectory of the result. The wise king Solomon reminded us "Death and life are in the power of the tongue: and they that love it shall eat the fruit thereof" (Proverbs 18:21 KJV). Bearing shame and guilt is more than enough to hold you hostage and block your future, but recovery and healing are in God's plan for your life. Every day you wake up to the same old thinking, your life seems to be stagnant, and filled with complexities. It becomes very difficult to get by; but that's okay, God is leading you through the process of "walk by faith and not by sight" (2 Corinthians 5:7). God wants you to turn the page to a new life. This new life begins with you—a new creation, a brand new you. Bill Gaither sang, "Something beautiful, something good. All my confusions, he understood. All I had to offer him was brokenness and strife, but he made something beautiful of my life". As you focus on the new path and maintain the brand new you, always be grateful and excited about life. Strengthen yourself and guard your mind to stand up and to turn away from the things that prevent you from gaining back your power in God; this is your breaking point. Speak over your life; keep pouring into your spirit for God has chosen you. Trust yourself, for you have committed yourself to God's will. You can have self-reliance through Christ Paul wrote, "I can do all things through Christ which strengthens me" (Philippians 4:13).

When you are empowered, nothing can stand in the way of your success. No devils, no witches, no iniquity workers, no satanic stronghold, and no demon possessed element can set you back, because you are protected under the blood of Jesus Christ. Move forward with confidence and focus on who you are; through faith you shall conquer and be victorious.

Confidence is a very powerful word. It is a booster to low self-esteem and embraces faith, purpose, and focus. It allows you to be irrevocable and unstoppable. Nothing can by any means move, or make you think less of who you are when you are confident. Be excited, be grateful to God who has loaded you up with talents and purposes for his will. God isn't finished with you, but rather, he is ready to use you. Issues may cause you to think of yourself as dysfunctional, but I repeat, God is not finished with you. Your status has been changed and your focus is empowered. You are not a prisoner in your own body; you are not set on the prisoner's bench. You now know how, and when, to dismiss the thoughts of satanic strategies. You are no pain to your own self; you are your own therapy. This is how you think with your Creator who changed your mindset. Now you can focus on the things that are spiritual, things that are eternal. Focus on the things that excite and enthuse. The woman didn't know that she was gifted and talented until she moved out of isolation and into the spotlight of faith; a faith that stands out in the hearts of mankind to this day. God loaded her up with self-confidence and self-control. These were not achieved overnight, but through faith and reliance.

Self-confidence, and self-control are tools for goal setting. Using these tools will enhance you and bring you into a better lifestyle of empowerment and focus on the Almighty God.

We do and will continue to experience challenging times, but we are human and that is to be expected. However, despite the situation, we must do our best while trusting in God to fill in the gaps and work on the rest.

The ability to focus is all managed by the mind. For example, for your prayer to be effective, you will have to pray sincerely and with true faith. Jesus said: "when we pray, we should believe that we receive what we asked of Him and shall have them" (Mark 11: 24). "All things are possible to him that believeth" (Mark 9: 23). "Draw near to God with a true assurance of faith" (Hebrews 10: 22).

James encourages us to ask of God wavering nothing. James 1: 6 says "But let him ask in faith, nothing wavering. For he that wavereth is like a wave of the sea driven with the wind and tossed". Wavering faith refers to the mind being unsettled, in between or unsure. God wants a faith that can work and move with him; especially when you hit rock bottom. It is imperative that you believe that he can bring you out through faith. For without faith it is impossible to please God (Hebrews 11:6). God is not partial. John 3: 16 says "For God so love the world that he gave his only begotten son that whosoever believeth in him should not perish but have everlasting life".

Jesus came to heal, deliver and set free. God uses you as his mouthpiece, so be generous to one another and get excited to tell someone of his favor and faithfulness toward you.

While I waited for my healing from God of my diseases, I knew it was a process and that it would take time, so I maintained my focus, I fasted, prayed, and read the word of God daily. I believed God's word as it is written to the letter. When I thought about all the healing miracles he had done in the bible days, I believed that if God had done it for others, he could and would do it for me. I dismissed negative thoughts going through my head, including the doubts and fear that I shall not pull through this situation. Each time I lay to rest the adversary came with something new to cause me to despair. I would repeat Scripture verses, I held on to faith with God's promises for my life, and repeated the words "Thank you, Jesus. Thank you, Jesus", until I fell asleep. I held on to Jacob's determination when he declared that he would not let go until God blessed him; I would not let go until God healed me. I saw the waves on the electro cardiogram machine move from abnormal to abnormal over a period of time. Today the doctors are asking that I don't ever report that I had a heart attacked. Thank God for my new heart. (Genesis

32:26). "Death is an appointment unto man," says the Scripture in Hebrew 9. Without controversy, death is a part of God's plan. In those moments I declared Psalm 118:17 over my life "I shall not die but live and declare the works of the Lord." Every day I lived I deemed it as a blessing. I lived and declared. If you allow the devil to get the best of you, he will let your mind feel sicker than what your tissues are experiencing. In other words, your mind is sicker than the physical body. So, I believe in faith, I speak in faith, I practice faith and I live by faith. I see faith as a very important tool in my life. "And not weak in faith, he considered not his own body now dead, when he was about a hundred years old, neither yet the deadness of Sarah's womb:" (Romans 4:19 KJV).

Exodus 15:26 says "If thou wilt diligently hearken to the voice of the Lord thy God, and wilt give ear to his commandments and keep all his statutes, I will put none of these diseases upon thee, which I have brought upon the Egyptians: for I am the Lord that healeth thee." To speak healing over my life I believed the work is done in Jesus's name. With God all things are possible, and his word declared that there is nothing too hard for him to do. Tell him you believe his Word, let God know that he is your great physician. God wants for your faith to meet his, and when faith meets faith, miracles takes place. Are you ready for your miracle? God is faithful to his promises. Hold on and don't let go you have too much waiting for you at the end of this season. Remember what you are praying for.

The devil will sometimes try to bring the issues back to your mind. He will even try to tell you that you are not healed. Satan is a full-time liar and you cannot allow him to have your mind. Satan is a spirit sending messages to your mind. Use mechanisms of faith, prayer and the Word of God to block him. Use your God-given sources to have good triumph over evil intentions. Satan's desire was for you to succumb to your issues; his desire is to rob, kill, and destroy you. Therefore, when he sees God raise you up, he is defeated, he is confused, and nervous because you are empowered with some real testimonies to "big up" your praise unto the Almighty God. God is already big, no one can make him bigger, but you can big up your praise.

For God is great and greatly to be praised. When we praise him this in turn adds fuel to our prayer life which keeps us focused and further unlocks even greater potentials in us. when you pray absent-mindedly, your prayer cannot be centered and is therefore ineffective. Maybe you were fearful, or tired to the point where you fell asleep while praying, or you have become repetitive while praying. We pray effectively when we pray in the spirit. When we pray, dark clouds must be removed through God's divine intervention; for you pray by faith and hope for your victory through faith. Don't be tricked by the master trickster who will tell you to lay down in the bed and pray or pray silently. That has not always been successful because most time you fall asleep without actually praying. However, when you go to God sincerely broken, giving room for cleansing and motives to be controlled, there will be a difference. It is not the amount of time you spend in prayer, but rather the sincerity of your approach to God.

The mind can be a battlefield, meaning that the mind is at war. According to Romans 7: 21 (KJV), "I find then a law, that, when I would do good, evil is present with me".

Isaiah 26: 3 says "Thou wilt keep, him in perfect peace, whose mind is stayed on thee: because he trusteth in thee".

Evil thoughts are trafficking, and so do good thoughts. Evil thoughts can be strong and very demanding and sometimes it may even feel as if the evil thoughts can overcome the good thoughts. An example in the Bible is of the eight fruits of the spirit and the nine fruits of the flesh in Galatians 5: 19–23.

Be encouraged. God's promises are unchangeable. The good thing is, he promises to keep you in perfect peace if your mind stays on him. It is impossible to avoid evil thoughts around us, but we can avoid being a partaker of evil thoughts. Through your Creator, you can maintain that positive peace even in times of strife or turmoil, because you pray to God by faith to dismiss the element of evil thoughts from your mind.

A positive focus is having an attitude that is steady and stable, supported by God and unchanging. It is said that negative emotions often result from focusing on mistakes of the past. If God has forgiven your sins, then there is no reason not to forgive yourself. One of the most difficult factors is to forgive yourself. However, rather than beating up on yourself, carrying the guilt of what we are ashamed of and living in tensions that make it harder for our tissues, known that God is always the way out. David had a hard time dealing with his guilt. Psalm 51: 3 (KJV) says, "For I acknowledge my transgression: and my sin is ever before me". David sought the Lord, his Creator, and God heard him and forgave him; David accepted God's forgiveness, and his loving mercies. He stepped past his guilt, stepped past the negatives and emotional setbacks, and allowed the Lord to reinstate his Christ-like lifestyle. "Then shalt thou be pleased with the sacrifices of righteousness, with burnt offering and whole burnt offering: then shall they offer bullocks upon thine altar" (Psalm 51:19). David focused on his forgiveness and reached out to God by faith for the healing of his mind. His difficult disposition was for God's purpose to be made manifested in him. Let your mind focus on your change, accept the new you. You are a miracle of yourself; just look where you were, and where you are today. It took faith to get you started and faith to get you here. You are victorious through faith. Thank God for victory through faith.

If at anytime you find yourself heading back into your destructive past, in Philippians 4: 8, Paul emphasized on some valuable factors that we should focus on, "whatsoever things are true, whatsoever things are honest, whatsoever things are just, whatsoever things are pure, whatsoever things are lovely, whatsoever things are of good report; if there be any virtue, and if there be any praise, think on these things." Paul expressed the reasons for self-denial. A true Christian behavioral setting is to concentrate on things eternal, the things that will keep your mind on Christian goals. We change our moral and ethical behavior by letting Christ live in us so that he can shape us into what we should be. Talk to God, he is your Christian strength. God has all the answers to each of your problems.

CHAPTER 5
Maximize Your Courage

The woman's central issue was her bleeding, her barriers were her rituals, and her fear was the ability to face the public. Her barriers denied her accessibility and narrowed her privilege; but courage overtook her desperate need. She maximized her courage. Although life was very difficult and risky, she was furnished with enough courage to keep her during difficult times.

Courage is a decision made to act despite fear or difficulties; it is a choice that must be made by you. When courage is instilled, it cannot be eradicated easily unless you allow it. What is planted in you will remain and grow if you maintain it.

Being home from the hospital started a new journey. I experienced limitations because of my issues, but I would not allow my issues o let me surrender to limitations. I was given a lot of do's and don'ts but I tried to push against limitations. I can't forget the day at the park with my two girls and my six weeks old son. I started feeling dizzy, my heart pounding as if it was coming out of my chest. Fear gripped me, I was scared and panicking to the point that I felt it was my last moment on earth.

I tried to hold it together, I said "God don't let me die here with my three young children with no one to help us we are here alone in the park". In that terrified moment, I gave my son to my eight years old daughter. It wasn't me any more but God leading. He led me to a cistern that I had scorned and told my children never to drink from that had become my refuge. After drinking the water, the pounding in my heart ceased, but I was still feeling nervous, weak, and afraid of how we would get home.

You can only imagine what took place here, Elysia eight years old with her six weeks old brother walking home about .25km while my six years old Lachane held onto my hand as we walked very gingerly home. As I reflex on the words of David: "I shall not die but live and declared the works of the Lord. My issues were overwhelming and brought me to a place of surrender. It seems as if my issues could not bear it any more. I believe God was testing me, but at that time I didn't understand he was taking me through my valley of the shadow of death, I thought we were alone at the park, but the angels of the Lord were there encamping around us. The devil also was there with the spirit of fear telling me that I would not be able to make it home alive, but I did make it home. It was then that I discovered that the devil was filled with lies, with a tongue of butter packed with generosity and possessing nothing.

God had a special task for Joshua to take immediate leadership after the passing of Moses. God saw potential, purpose, and destiny in Joshua. God promoted him from being a minister to a leader and God charged him, "Be strong and of good courage: for unto this people shall thou divide for the inheritance of the land. Which I swear unto their fathers to give them" (Joshua 1:6).

After being given the mantle of leadership, God also encouraged Joshua, "Only be thou strong and very courageous, that thou mayest observe to do according to all the law, which Moses my servant commanded thee: turn not from it to the right hand or to the left mayest thou prosper whithersoever thou goest" (Joshua 1:7). Joshua maximized his courage and moved in the strength of the Lord, and God led him graciously and successfully. Territorial walls were torn down, lands were captured, enemies were defeated, and victory was won. Joshua had no leadership experience; rather he was a follower of Moses (minister), but the moment God placed leadership in him, God maximized his courage to deal with the disobedient and rebellious people in his days.

At some point in time, the woman with the issue of blood discovered that various healing had taken place where Jesus was concerned and based upon that result, she maximized her courage, purposed in her heart that this day she would take her healing by force. She did not care for the crowd and what people might have said, or even care if the blood came running down her feet. She was determined and courageous with her moves.

Difficult situations that never seem to have an end may try to overthrow your courage, but God wants you to eradicate your fear and boost your courage. If you remain in your isolated disposition it will not change your past. You can push past your circumstances, take risks, accept failure if it comes, just don't dwell on it, it is just a path to success. You have been there and done that. There is no reason to get back into it. "For forward still it's Jehovah's will through the billows dash and spray with a conquering thread we will push ahead and roll the sea away".

You have come too far to be defeated by fear. Fear is always that monster in the way, ready to scare the life out of you. It is not real; do not let it get to you by trying to dictate or to control your emotions in any way. It is like ticks in your tissues, sucking your blood. You are an overcomer! Challenge your fear by maximizing your courage and you will come out alive and take charge of what God has called you to do. God has called you and appointed you with a meaningful gift. You are gifted and appointed by God.

What you need to know is that your gift is not for the four corners of the walls, it is not a souvenir to be placed in a treasure box, but it is to come alive in you. The anointing that God placed in you is amazingly powerful. Let it flow inside out, someone else needs to know how to get where you are. Jesus wants you to be their navigator. What do you have to offer? What help have you for society? Is there any passion for souls, passion to volunteer in your community, passion to be an inspiration to others, passion to reach out to the poor and needy? Fear must go, it is a hindrance and it is now time to maximize courage and move to the next level. You are resilient and your faith is strong despite what the devil tells you. Dismiss those thoughts from your mind. The Lyrics of Mrs. E. E. Williams say, "Tho' the garden lies before me, and the scornful judgment hall Tho' the gloom of deepest midnight settles around me like a pall; Darkness cannot affright me never, From thy presence shadows flee, and if thou guide me ever, Jesus, I'll go thro' with thee. Tho' the earth may rock and tremble, tho' the sun may hide its face, tho' my foes be strong and ruthless, still I dare to trust thy grace; Tho' the cross may overshadow, thou didst bear it once for me and what e'er the pain or peril, Jesus, I'll go through with thee."

The woman was a woman of the covenant, she was born into it and subject to it, and therefore, she had to deal with it. You control your issue, do not let your issue control you. You control your anger, temper and all behavioral issues. If you let it get the best of you, it will only embarrass you. Become master of your issues and it will make you more intelligent. The beauty of self-encouragement is taking care of you first, then being empowered to take care of those you love while understanding that God is using you as a beacon of strength and motivation for others when they find themselves in difficult times. You can inspire others who have their head hanging down to the ground; you can bring them back to the height of their dreams and even beyond.

Think out of the box and move beyond your feelings. Feelings will block your interest, set back your courage, and use up your decision-making skill. Do not think less of who you are; trust yourself because you are bigger than what is going through your mind right now. You are observant, optimistic, and creative. You are the person God wants to use. You are no substitute; you are chosen for this purpose; don't let your mind get the best of you.

You have worked too hard to let your diplomas, and certificates be eaten by dust. Think of all the sleepless nights and weary days, the exams, the prayers, the fasting, the dedication, and the financial expenses. You have too much to gain to lose. Build up your courage and maximize your search for where your interest is. Do not give up on yourself because you have what it takes; it is not about where you want to go, but about where God is about to take you. Be courageous and maximize your faith. Sometimes we make the wrong decisions, but it is important to learn how to respond to your fear. It can approach you without warning, but don't be overthrown by your mistakes.

It is so amazing how Jesus flips the coin to bring about equality. Should we embark on this ritual, our chances of survival would be very slim, but luckily, all praise and glory be to our God who searched out the universe and found one person who was willing to commit for this purpose. That God would use her to bring about changes that others would not. She fit in perfectly, like a missing puzzle piece; a woman who had no family, who had no name, no friends, or fame, but had an aim; believing that God could bring her from imperfection to perfection.

The innkeeper said there was no room in the inn, what the Innkeeper did not realize was that, in a way, the inn was not big enough to accommodate baby Jesus. They did not know how to maximize their courage nor faith, so they thought they had refused him. However, Jesus has refused them; he encompassed wisdom and power that was beyond their imagination. Yet this same Jesus became so small, enough to live in our hearts. Is there any room in your inn for Jesus? Please let him in. There was trouble in the inn, there was segregation in the inn, and there was conservation. Jesus wants you to humble yourself as you maximize your courage to face disappointments, to face up with the scrutinizers, the false teachers, and with hypocritical behaviors, often from people close to you. God is great and greatly to be praised. He is mighty in power; he uses the basic things of this world to amaze man, to let man understand that there is none like him. He is not an imitator; he is God all by himself. No one found him, but he found us, change our behaviors and wayward minds and made us into something good.

This woman was not beloved, she was despised and forsaken by her culture, so God used her to change the setting and operation of her culture. Jesus may use you to preach a sermon; he may allow you to use objects or people to demonstrate the actual thing in you. What God is downloading in your spirit is so powerful that sometimes it is hard to explain the mystical things of the anointing power in a way that your audience may find understanding.

ISSUES IN THE TISSUES

God's power is blind to human understanding until God brings out the spiritual to the natural. Jesus used this woman as an instrument to demonstrate to the universe that he has the power to do all things. Jesus flipped the coin to bring out his purpose. When you are burdened down with ongoing issues, it is often difficult to understand what's taking place in your tissues. Maximize your courage, your faith, and your patience. It is only a matter of time before God flips your coin. When Jesus flipped the coin he said, "Daughter". Calling her daughter made a big difference in her life. What a difference it makes when Jesus makes the change. He takes care of the issues in your tissues and I guarantee you, he will change your life around.

The woman exercised her courage as she stood in the time of her adversity. She built courage around her issues and she stood faithfully, never revolting through her rough times, pain, loneliness, isolation, and her physical and emotional imprisonment. She lacked human contact and communication as she may not have had any family members or friends. Her disposition labeled her lifestyle and her lifestyle was worse than being a slave; her lying down and her rising up was embarrassing. Understand that she could not have sat on chairs, as a matter of a fact she could not have sat on any kind of furniture as she desired, because her bleeding was like a fountain flowing inside out. Jesus showed up just in time, surely his feelings has been touched with our infirmities. Suddenly, this woman's private life went viral. Jesus allowed her miraculous healing to impact many lives. There was no point hiding her healing. Jesus empowered her with faith that conquered fear. When Jesus heals and delivers you, there is a joy deep down inside. So much so that you can't keep it to yourself; somebody else should know about the supernatural power of Jesus Christ.

The bible speaks of the blind man. This man who was healed by the power of Jesus could not keep his healing to himself, although he was pressured by the people not to speak of the power of Jesus Christ.

He had his issues from birth, his blindness was no secret to the people, but they did not believe in the miraculous works that Jesus performed. The young man maximized courage, moved with perseverance, and faced up to the crowd. When God maximize your faith, faith begins to increase, along with your courage and will to persevere. When these collaborate, when these join forces, you will bring down the satanic kingdom. Your faith, courage and perseverance have the strength to combat the enemy and defeat his purposes. Imagine, even the devil has a purpose; his purpose is to fight against the people of God, to twist things around to attract and attack the minds of believers. You are not a weakling. You now know how to join forces, to arm yourself with the Word of God, to fight and win. "For we wrestle not against flesh and blood, but against principalities, against powers, against the rulers of the darkness of this world, against spiritual wickedness in high place. Wherefore take unto you the whole armor of God, that ye may be able to withstand in the evil day, and having done all, to stand" (Ephesians 6:12–13)

This is the preparation for war! It can be somewhat daunting when we come face to face with unexpected attacks which can have you feeling unprepared and like a soldier deployed but unarmed. No one likes defeat, but you are not a quitter so don't give up or give in. You have the courage to stand.

The anonymous woman came out of her hiding place, not caring about what anyone said or thought of her, willing to face the whatever repercussions there were for her being out in public. She was dressed in courage; she stepped out by faith and moved with preservation. She came out of isolation, shook off her fears, and claimed her freedom. When doubt arose, she strangled it, refusing to give in and let it define her; it was now Jesus over issues. When you come to that place in your mind where it is Jesus over your problems, then you are seasoned, and your mind is set on God, being assured that only Jesus can fix the situation. Moses believed that God was able to build a relationship with the children of Israel, but the children of Israel had mixed thoughts about whether their Creator was going to deliver them. What the children of Israel did not know was that God was going to give them a breakthrough from the hands of Pharaoh. It was at their breakthrough that Pharaoh's host went after the children of Israel even up until the Red Sea. The Red Sea was their barrier and it was there that Moses had to maximized courage and demonstrated God's power. The children of Israel saw Moses as their shepherd, so they all went to Moses seeking answers for their safety. Israel had forgotten that God had established his covenant with them, to give them the land of Canaan, the land of their pilgrimage, wherein there were strangers (Exodus 6: 4-5 KJV).

The Red Sea was only a set-up for their deliverance. When God delivered them, God said that these enemies that they see today will not be seen by them anymore (Exodus 14:13). Understand here, deliverance is not a breakthrough neither is your break through your deliverance. If you are delivered from your issues, it will not return unto you a second time. Nahum 1:9 says, "whatever they plot against the Lord He will bring to an end; trouble will not come a second time." In other words, you have been delivered. When you were in need of a financial breakthrough to pay off some debts, you prayed, and you got your breakthrough. However, because it was a breakthrough, before long you were back at the same page; your issues returned. That was a breakthrough. When God delivers you, it shall not return to you a second time. The woman did not receive a breakthrough, but she was delivered.

CHAPTER 6
Endure to Succeed

Endure to succeed. We generally use these words of Paul "God will not give you more than you can bear" (1 Corinthians 10:13). God always gives solutions in every situation. If he brings you into it, he will bring you through it. If you can't cure the situation, endure it. God allowed strange things to happen to you to bring out unique experiences. God is mystical, and his miraculous power cannot be hidden, it must be made manifest in you that others will acknowledge that your Creator does reign. You are only human and that is what makes you so unique. Your Creator becomes your investor; he wants to invest in you to bring out the image he has created.

God knows how frail you are; he knows you would be faced with problematic situations that no human can resolve. He knows about the issues before it gets into the tissues. He removes the blockage and the root cause while processing your brain to bring freedom to your mind. When the mind is clogged, it cannot function the way it should. He works on the invisible and brings out the visible.

God's intention is to bring you to perfection. As only God is perfect, it takes the perfectness of God to bring the imperfect to perfection. God is willing to work with you no matter how long it takes. God will endure with you until you succeed. He sees you as his candidate; he sees steadfastness in you and is about to bring you to some strange places, places you have never been before. Philippian 3: 9-10 says, "And be found in him, not having mine own righteousness, which is of the law but that which is through the faith of Christ, the righteousness which is of God by faith: That I may know him, and the power of his resurrection, and the fellowship of his sufferings, being made conformable unto his death". God is taking you out of your comfort zone, not to confuse you but to mesmerize you, to show you the mysteries of God, and the purpose of your calling. You have what it takes to be his candidate. He has delighted in you. There is more to you than you can see. If you endure in God you will succeed.

With the willingness of heart, God will use you to bring out his purpose in you, even in situation like Daniel's. Daniel endured under pressure and became successful in his determination. That is where your decision-making skills become useful. When you are placed under pressure, will you endure the test and succeed in the plans God has for you? God has placed some lion-hearted men and women in your presence to prove you. How could a loving God allow such a dramatic thing to happen? Tests are important. God is processing you and training you for greater tasks ahead, to bring out his purpose in you. Watch God shut the hungry, angry, and fierce lion's mouth, to boost your faith and strengthen your testimonies, to make unbelievers astonished at the mighty work of God. He can make workplace barriers and restrictions to be removed, for fierce and unkind bosses to be submissive and respectful to you, for co-workers/associates to be God-fearing in your presence because you have a holy God present in you who need to be reverenced. You have enough power to subdue, defeat, and declare your God-given right wherever you go. You shall not go under but you shall prevail and succeed.

You are faithful and your God will fight for you. Co-workers shall not overtake you, your boss will not overtake you, the principals will not overtake you, your neighbors will not overtake you, and bullies will not overtake your children. God will bring down the high places, keep their emotions under control, and allow them to surrender to you at God's command. Just watch God keep them under his control. You will not go under; the Lord is on your side. When the enemies turn up the heat, Jesus steps in like a mighty army to defend you and disappoint the enemies. You are covered with his blood; you shall not by any means be defeated.

Whatever you are experiencing, give it to Jesus, it is for his glory. The songwriter said, "He's a friend that well-known". Jesus knows that there would be cares of life, he knows the weaknesses of humanity as well as our emotions, he knows that human beings are subject to fail without him. Jesus gave an easy solution to control issues in the tissues that make us cumbered, 1 Peter 5:7 (KJV) says, "Casting all your cares upon him; for he careth for you". God did not categorize or put a limit on what he would do. God said to give all your cares and concerns to him. When your troubles come, don't be fearful, just give it to God. For something that is beyond your comprehension, give it to Jesus, when financial complexities come, give it to him. The Bible states, "and the cattle upon a thousand hills" are his (Psalm 50:10). That is more than enough of an assurance in the Lord. Life complexities may bombard you, but you shall not fear because you know how to endure.

The anonymous woman was committed to her restriction because it was her daily routine. Her blood flowing issues were always her barrier, however, she had to stick with her impossibilities until her possibilities came forth. Through all that she was experiencing, God had her at heart. Even if she had felt discouraged, succumbing to her issues was not an option. Jesus knew her destiny and her destiny would not have been pre-mature or over-processed. Jesus allowed her to endure to succeed. She was making the path more accessible for you and me. With incredible focus and determination, she endured to the end. Her determination superseded her issues. The issues in the tissues were subdued while faith prevailed.

You are an overcomer, you have determination, you know how to pray, you know how to wait on God, and you know what it means to be committed. You are a successor of faith through your forefather Abraham, you know that God is depending on you to work through you.

In our Christian environment, we are subject to certain restrictions that governed the church. The church is subject to doctrine, rules, and regulations. The church is here to make a difference to unbelievers, not only for their physical needs, but also to take care of the holistic needs. Each is entitled to their belief and their faith as God will do all the necessary changes. In 1 John 2:15-17 (KJV) it states:

> "Love not the world, neither the things that are in the world. If any man loves the world, the love of the father is not in him. For all that is in the world, the lust of the flesh, and the lust of eyes, and the pride of life is not of the father, but of the world. And the world passeth away, and the lust thereof: but he that doeth the will of God abideth forever".

Being lonely, her Jehovah—Shammah appeared in her weakness, and her Jehovah-Rapha brought healing, strength, and comfort to her tissues.

I believe she was praying to her Creator as she awaited the coming of her Messiah. She had no means, no other hope. The hymnology sings, "When all around my soul gives way, he then is all my hope and stay". God enriched her with the power of endurance, which took her to a higher level of trust and confidence in God; her solution was to believe. Humanly, there were moments when she might have said, "Lord if you have kept me these twelve years to the present, my condition may not be pleasant now, but I believe you're going to make my life better. Help me to trust you." God was her only way of communication. "Alone with God and in him hidden to hold with him communion sweet," says the hymnology. God empowered her with endurance to navigate her through her difficult and unpleasant process. For a long period of twelve years, despite the fatigue and the stressful moments she faced, endurance was one of her priorities. Succeed to endure.

God wants you to endure and to succeed, so he furnished you with tools to pursue, through God who strengthens you. You can master the activities of your task. When you become committed to God's will, no power from hell can hold you back.

No matter how chaotic your surroundings get, or how challenging it appears, God will allow you to tolerate, to manage, whatever comes. God sees you as his masterpiece; he knows you are resourceful and filled with purpose and He can use you to demonstrate his power. In so doing, others can see that God dwells inside of you. God has equipped you with strategies and resources, equipped you for greatness, and he lives and reigns in your life. He is supreme! No matter what life demands of you, God has the best for you. It does not matter how intense your issues get, God has already boosted your emotions, healed your tissues and given peace to your mind.

We all go through day-to-day struggles and encounter unexplainable circumstances. The path won't always be smooth, you will encounter some rough patches as well. There will be sicknesses, aches, and pain, but do not be terrified when these issues appear. It may not be what you have bargained for, but it is a part of life. We were born into it, and therefore are subject to it. We have to deal with the hurdles that come our way. Hurdles are traps to hinder success. This often bring feelings of fear or apprehension about what is to come; it may even try to stop you from doing the things that mean the most to you. It is only a mind thing; don't forget you control your mind and not your mind controlling you. You are destined to succeed. Every day Jesus is doing something new and he is about to do something new in your life. Show the world that even when life seems hopeless, they too can overcome by committing to God's will; you are destined to succeed.

God miraculously has you on his winning team and you didn't even know it. God does not need your approval, he has made preparation and chosen you for his potential purpose. His preparation must be complete. Listen, before an athlete can join the ranks of the greats in their chosen sport/industry, there are certain goals that need to be set and achieved. The mind must go through the process of plotting and planning, setting the expectations, possibilities, resources, and skills necessary to achieve the set goal. Hard work, purpose, commitment, patience, and perseverance/endurance are the necessary skills you have to move with potential and to be successful.

God's will for you is to endure even though your path gets "rough and tough" with the day-to-day intricacies of life. He supplies you with patience to help you along the way, proceed with caution and stay on the path. Isaiah 40 29–31 states, "He giveth power to the faint; and to them that have no might he increaseth strength. Even the youths shall faint and be weary, and the young men shall utterly fall: But they that wait upon the Lord shall renew their strength they shall mount up with wings as eagles; they shall run, and not be weary; they shall walk, and not faint." You are running God's marathon, and this is where eagerness meets potential. Eagerness is an entity that must be controlled. Being eager will put you into overdrive and will burn out your energy. The symptoms of being burned out are tiredness, frustration, confusion, and loss of focus. Put on your running shoes and run with dignity; run this race with purpose, with confidence, run for your healing deliverance, run for the ultimate prize, which is heaven. You are never a loser and no friend or foes can stop you. Defeat is not a part of the race, so run to succeed. You are almost there, you have made it, you must succeed.

Who said you would not make it? When God chose you as his candidate, he saw purpose in you. Take the limits off your purpose; God has authorized you above all limitations.

What is 'speech impediment'? It is a disorder that is commonly known as a stammer or stutter. This issue disrupts communication. A few of the symptoms are: embarrassment when speaking (not sure you are going to say the right thing), not making eye contact, and a love to write as a way of getting their words across. That being said, there are a lot of authors with a speech disorder. One prime biblical example is Moses who wrote the first five books of the Bible, of the Old Testament, which include the books from Genesis to Deuteronomy. Moses conquered his fear by doing God's task. Moses saw limitations, but God saw purpose, qualification, and leadership. Moses's big issue was his speech impediment. He thought he wouldn't be able to carry out his task as God's Messenger. Fear was dictating to his intelligence. Moses conquered fear when God asked, "who made the mouth, who made tongue, I will send you Aaron" (Exodus 4:11). God did send Aaron but only to assist Moses, not to do his task. Even when you feel that you are not qualified for a position because of fear, trust that if God places you in it, he will furnish you with all the necessary skills to perform it.

I had been a victim of this issue since I was a child; I had some struggles with stammering. Fear had dictated me, fear had me down and tried to hold me back. Today, I manage my fear and do not let fear manage me. A little stuttering in my thoughts would be internalized as I struggled with fear to bring it out. Fear will let you think you didn't do a good job, that you are not eloquent enough make you feel inadequate. I had been there, I had struggled with stuttering to the point where I felt so embarrassed, I hung my head down while communicating, I would literally make no eye contact hoping that the conversation would quickly come to an end and my words would be very few. Today I look back and smile at some of my struggles. How had I let fear hold me back? God had spoken to me many times to do his task, but when I become hesitant, instantly someone else would step forward and do the task. Feeling so ashamed, I would repent to God. Fear had me down. Today I have conquered my fear through God; I may still have a little stuttering here and there, but fear is no longer that big giant staring back at me.

When I go for my walk in the mornings, I don't just go for walks, but I walk for a cause, with someone on my mind. Praying for someone's deliverance, victory, divine healing; praying to break forces and subdue enemies. When I leave the house, I go through the door with somebody's situation. I give it to God and leave it in the atmosphere; I tell God I'm not going back home with it. Walking is a great way to communicate and build up your relationship with your Creator. He wants to teach you how to endure around others circumstances so that they too may know how to get over their issues.

In 2 Timothy 2:3-4 (KJV) it says, "Thou, therefore, endure hardness, as a good soldier of Jesus Christ. No man that warreth entangleth himself with the affairs of this life; that he may please him who hath chosen him to be a soldier." A solder that is deployed for battle is not guaranteed to return home to his families and love ones; realistically he has a job to do and he must get it done, dead or alive. You are on The battlefield to fight, however fight to win. The conflict gets heated but you are not afraid. That is expected, your alternate purpose is to succeed. God has fully equipped you, not with the "helmet of brass or armed with coat of mail" as the Philistine did to Goliath, (1 Samuels 17:43-45). Jesus equipped you, "Above all taking the shield of faith wherewith ye shall be able to quench all the fairy darts of the wicked. And take the helmet of Salvation, and the sword of the spirit, which is the word of God:" (Ephesians 6:16-17). Put on the whole armor.

The unknown woman was simply unique in her own way, but what else could she have done but to be faithful to God and believe? A worst-case scenario would be to find yourself in a disposition that held you hostage, to feel that life is over for you, the worst result is to be kicked to the curb. If God should think the way we do and act the way we do, life would be hopeless and would not be worthwhile fighting for. But because he is God and his love has been extended to all generation, he isn't obligated to you, rather he loves you beyond your condition or obligation. God's love is unconditional. God only wants you to endure to succeed.

As I reminisce and look at my son today and see where God has brought him from, I can see that three weeks old baby lying in his cot beside me in the hospital. I Was restricted from breast feeding my son due to possibly side-effects that may occurs from the radiation. I struggled to express the milk from my breast to be stored to feed my baby. Each drop of milk gave me a dash of hope as I held on to faith that I will be healed and live to see my only son grow up. I did not want to die and leave my children, especially my baby. My heart ached as the nurses tried to let me hold him. During my family's visitation, I would hold back tears, but as soon as they left the room river tears would flow down my cheeks and soak my pillow. My speech was in impaired, I could not communicate effectively to my family due to the medical ventilator for oxygen and high blood pressure which held me between a rock and a hard place. I had visitation and phone calls restriction, except for my immediate family who still had limited visitations.

CHAPTER 7
Returning to a Situation is Not the Solution

Returning to a situation is not the solution.

The children of Israel had a concern about their new way of living in the wilderness. Though they were not disdained as they were in the land of Egypt, they rebelled and murmured against Moses and Aaron. They thought returning to a life style of Egypt would have been a better solution.

That was a way of God testing the children of Israel, to humble them. God had some better things in store for them, but their issues were un-gratefulness and disobedience. Their physical body was out of the land of Egypt, but psychologically their minds were still there. God had better plans for them, but they couldn't see a better country, a better lifestyle, and a better future for their lives. The devil had distracted their minds and blindfolded their spiritual eyes. He had their mind fixed on their current situations, and not on their long-term goal, which God had made a promise unto them.

Understand here, after spending over four hundred years in bondage, being enslaved by their taskmasters, I believe God was saying to them, "You are my children, the apple of my eyes. You have suffered enough; you have slaved enough, and I have heard your cry. This is your season, enjoy your change of environment, this is not all because the best is yet to come. Only obey my laws and walk in my statues and I will take care of you". God's mandate is "freedom from bondage" (Numbers 11:10).

We all have our testimonies, how God delivered us from the bondage of sin, ten years for me was more than enough time slaving for the devil, but thanks be to God, he delivered me right on time. God defended my freedom and gave me a one-track mind.

You are too smart, you will not be defeated by the devil's tricks, neither will you be distracted by his wicked devices, or his smooth words to charm or entice you. I would like to awaken your memory to my previous statement, that the devil is a thief with a tongue of butter, packed with genericity and possessing nothing. You are wise and you know when his presence is around. You are an overcomer. You will not fall victim to his cunning craftiness of the oppressor because God gave you a one-track mind as his believer. Margaret Jenkins Harris put these words together in her, refrain "You need not to look for me, down in Egypt's sand, for I have pitched my tent far up in Beulah land; you need not to look for me, down in Egypt's sand, for I have pitched my tent far up in Beulah land."

The woman with her issue of blood was free from being enslaved, and without conservation had no need to return to her imprisonment. Her faith had made her whole, and her faith had promoted her as "daughter," as well as to the status of a faithful and progressive human being living a normal life. She was no longer afraid of being stone, and had no more oppressive thoughts or feelings of shame and embarrassment. God had removed all her obstacles and replaced them with freedom through faith.

According to Hebrews 11:15-16, the saints of the Old Testament died with faith, believing that God had some better things in store for them. While they lived, they didn't see the final promised blessing of the redeemed. The basic hope was eternal life with God in the heavenly homeland, and they fixed their eyes on their citizenship which is to come. "And truly, if they had been mindful of that country, from whence they came out, they might have had the opportunity to have returned. But now they desire a better country, that is, a heavenly: wherefore God is not ashamed to be called their God: for he hath prepared for them a city".

Relapse is not a part of the plan that God has for your life. His desire is for you to get beyond the mistakes. We all make mistakes, whether great or small, but you can be successful despite your past. Stop blaming yourself for mishaps. Things do happen, just don't dwell on them. God wants you to put them behind you and give yourself another chance while he is giving many chances. Every moment is valuable and so are you. Never think of yourself as less important in your world view. Be excited about life, that is all you have in this world. The rich man might be struggling, not because of money but because of poor health. When the rich man's issues begin to destroy the tissues, you see tears of sorrow and misery and discomfort because they hate to say goodbye to a lifestyle of luxury. It is life over wealth and not wealth over life. When you have life, you have everything to make you wealthy and your life worth living.

Every now and then you need to do a review to see what your next move is; to see what else is needed for the next level. You may need to re-energize, reboot, refresh, and re-vamp. You know how to turn a new page and create a change; you know how to execute and navigate, to move from hopeless to hopefulness, from setback to liberation, from impossibilities to possibilities. God breaks all limitations.

Who told you God had given up on you? Absolutely not! He only wants you to give him your will. He is just about to turn your life around, but one thing missing is your will. God's will is divine, so when he takes your stubborn will, he molds it to his. Your then stubborn will becomes his perfect will. God wants your mind to be focused on him. Claim your mind, your peace, your will. These are great attributes and they are yours; they are your tools. You cannot work without your mind, your peace, and your will. You have power over these issues, they will not stick to your tissues. You have the power to subdue and defeat all spirits that are not of God. Have God's protection over your precious gems; if they become messed up you will be dysfunctional. Let God's anointing power protect your mind.

If only you could see Jesus from your world view and imagine the plans he has for your life. He has a package with your name tagged on it. You just need to maximize your faith to achieve what God has promised you. According to the Miami Mass Choir "What

God has for me, it is for me, it is for me, I know without a doubt that He will bring me out; what God has for me is for me." You know that God is real and for you to prove him you need to speak thing into existence and expect it to happen with faith, believing. Excel for greatness.

Going back to the former things is not the solution. Romans 8:28-29 states, "And we know that all things work together for good to them that love God, to them who are called according to his purpose. For whom he did foreknew, he also predestinates to be conformed to the image of his son, that he might be the firstborn among many brethren. Moreover, whom he did predestinate, them he also called, and them he also justified, and whom he justified, them he also glorified." Let, no devil deceive you. You belong to God; he has chosen you. He has put his blood mark all over you, which is why you are so attractive to the enemy. So, the news is, you cannot go back to the way you use to be. The big decision is, he foreknew you. He called you and predestined you, and you are God's perfect candidate.

The unknown was unparalleled. She was miraculously healed from the inside out, she went from tests to triumphs, and from triumphant to viral. Her destiny was filled with purpose, but she was trapped by restrictions yet remained faithful in her circumstances. God needs faithful men and women to work for him. Men and women who are determined to stand through in difficult times, men and women who are willing to defend the faith, to be mentors for young men and young women, to be of example and encourage others along the way. You may feel unsuitable, but God saw possibility and purpose. He looked beyond your impossibilities and brought out purpose. Don't think bout what you are capable of, think what God can do, even if he must allow you to see with your natural eyes to believe that he is, like Thomas (John 20: 29).

God didn't call you or use you because you are perfect, but he called you and used you because he saw purpose in you.

Some of our setbacks today are caused by the spirit of fear. We allow fear to abuse our mind and disable our willpower, but I implore you today to take back your willpower and do the work your Creator designed for your life. Always think the best of yourself and have confidence in what you do. You know what you have prayed about; hasn't it manifested before your eyes? Yet you are still in doubt. Don't doubt when you can't understand; ask God for clarity. Doubt is a hindrance that wants to keep you back. When God says arise, fear says sit. When God says open your mouth and give praise fear says no someone is watching you. So, what if someone is watching? That is the devil's trick to get you distracted. Just forget about your surrounding and worship God. Fear is a big issue; it stands in the way of your progress, a wedge between you and your God, blocking your decision. Fear is your Jordan. You have a decision to make today, fear shall not be a monster before you anymore, stand in the power of faith, and call fear by its name. "Spirit of Fear you must go in Jesus name, my mind belongs to God. There is no place for you; I war against you by the blood of Jesus Christ. I decree and declare from this day forward you will not stand in the way of my success, in the way of my worship, in the way of my praise, nor in the way of my blessings in Jesus's name." You have enough power in you to order fear out of your life.

God is all powerful, Almighty, Omnipotent, this God lives inside of you. You know that God lives in you, you just prayed to him and asked of his favor. He has told you that you are blessed and highly favored of him. Just have confidence, he loves you, and he is your sustainer, your keeper and deliverer. He has brought you out of your situation not to hesitate, but to get started. His expectation is for you to remain in his will, to a greater inheritance of His promises. These are the words of Henry J. Gilmour "I'll tell of the pit, with its gloom and despair, I'll praise the dear Father, who answered my prayer; I'll sing my new song, the glad story of love, Then join in the chorus with the saints above".

When God saw that the children of Israel's minds were detouring, God had to remind them how he "brought them out of Egypt on Eagles Wings" (Exodus 19:4 KJV). It's okay to be reminded or else we fall back in our old ways.

The solution becomes an issue when we make a bad decision. Jesus said two roads are before you, make your choice. There is hell, and there is heaven. Very detailed, isn't it? Heaven leads to life everlasting and hell everlasting damnation. The option is up to humanity. Your decision matters, if your choice should be hell, the end is death, living in agony and consumed with fire. To be controlled by Satan when he himself will be burned, would be a very sad choice. Heaven is a place of everlasting joy, peace, and happiness, where you will live with God for evermore. The walls are said to be made of jasper, the streets of pure gold. It is an amazing expectation for the believers who love God and abide in his will. You know how to make the right choice, the right decision, how to ask God's leading and directions.

The woman may not have known why she was waiting, or what would have been her next move, but I do believe that God gave her a deep settled peace in the hardcore of her issues; a mind to deal with whatever was taking place in her tissues. How dare to question your Creator with whys, what, or the how's or to point fingers at others who are not walking in the will of their Creator? You have been chosen for his will to be manifested in you, that his glory might be revealed to unbelievers. We are his witness and bare His testimonies.

You are his true identity, the splitting image of your Creator and cannot be mistaken for the wrong identity. You have been born again, born of the water, the spirit and the blood. The blood of Jesus Christ is the proof of sonship, not from the blood of slain animals, that antidote was too weak for the cleansing of sin. You now carry God's DNA.

God's plan for the woman with her issues wasn't a mistake in identity, but a plan delivered to her by God. Whatever your Creator has in store for your life must be accomplished. It was God's plan for John to be placed on the Island of Patmos; there God flipped the coin of life over death. John couldn't have died according to the plan God had for his life. For a man to receive the revelation of the Lord Jesus Christ of the things that shall come to pass, if John was eaten by some sea mammals then the purpose, destiny, patience, and endurance would not have been fulfilled in Revelation.

Adam and Eve came up with a solution of running (escape) or hiding because of sin. They couldn't hide from God. God knew all about Adam as he was the image of God. God called Adam by the name "Adam! Where art thou?" (Genesis 3:9). David himself said, "whether shall I flee from thy presence" (Psalm 139:7).

You will not fall back into that old habit, that old path of hate, unforgiveness, depression and confusion, but rather navigate your way back to God's solution. His solution is for you to get closer to him. What can you do for God to use you? Help others who are heading down the wrong path you had once walked. You are the one God placed his plan in, your identity speaks for itself. You may try to run but cannot; you may try to hide but cannot. Returning back to a situation is absolutely not the solution, turn to God instead.

The devil tried to shift my faith, wanting me to return to my previous state I thought it was the devil's plans for my leg injuries, but the bible declared Psalm 91:11-12 For he shall give his angels charge over thee, to keep thee in all thy ways. They shall bear thee up in their hands, lest thou dash thy foot against a stone. Now I come to realized that God went into his treasure to place more investment in me. Sometimes my tissues were worn with issues, and the aches and pains seemed unbearable to the point that one night I asked my husband and my daughter Elysia to put me out on the porch. For a minute they thought I was going out of mind because it was one of the coldest nights in February. They hesitated. The more they hesitated the more I cried because of discomfort in my tissue, and so they eventually got me on the porch. At this time, it was now cold over pain. Emotionally, I felt better but psychically my tissues felt worse. The physiotherapy didn't work well for me that day because of my treatment. There was tingling in both legs by the time I got home, standing was very challenging for me even with aid of my crutches, and I later found out they had given me the wrong treatment. It should have been cold towel instead of hot towel as the cold towel would normally soothe the pain and reduce the swelling and inflammation in my tissues. However, despite this, I was persuaded that returning to that situation was absolutely not the solution, but to turn to God instead. I said, no aches or pain would stop me from going forward.

CHAPTER 8

Controlling the Issues in the Tissues

According to the scriptures, we are the image of God. To quote Genesis 1:26-27: "And God said, Let us made man in our own image, after our likeness: and let them have dominion over the fish of the sea, and over the fowl of the air, and over the cattle, and over all the earth, and over: every creeping thing that creepeth upon the earth. So, God created man in His own image, in the image of God created He him; male and female created him them."

As the image of God, we are made up of body, soul, and spirit; you are a special gift from God. The Scripture teaches that our Creator's intention for mankind is to experience an intimate relationship with God. Therefore, God created a human being as a unit both mortal, which is the physical, and immortal which is nonphysical. The soul and the spirits intellect, will, conscience, mind, and emotion are untouchable, because they are nonphysical. The great significance of the soul is that it never dies but exists endlessly beyond the life span of the psychical body. The physical body will decay and go back to the earth. Because it is earthy. Numbers 16:22 says, "And they fell upon their faces, and said, O God, the God of the spirit of all flesh, shall one-man sin, and wilt thou be wroth with all the congregation?" If we are in this psychical body, we are subject to issues in the tissues, disease and weakness.

Adam and Eve were challenged, as well as pressured by the devil, although they had an inner awareness of God's guidelines. Their conscience didn't prevail while being attacked by the devil. The personality concerning God's righteousness, and because of the wrongness of their actions they died a spiritual death; they accepted wrong over righteousness. The Scripture clearly states that:

> "Now the serpent was more subtil than the beast of the field which the Lord God had made. And he said unto the woman, Yea, hath God said, ye shall not eat of every tree of the garden? And the woman said unto the serpent, we may eat of the fruit of the garden: But of the fruit of the tree which is in the midst of the garden, God hath said, ye shall not eat of it neither shall he touch it, lest ye die." (Genesis 3:1-3)

Here the devil used his psychological deceptive skills and immediately the issue of confusion attacked the mind of Eve which contagiously transferred to Adam. It entered his system aggressively and he had no time to think of God's do's and don'ts, no time for rejection. Unfortunately, this disease spread like wildfire and is still on the rise up to this day.

This is the intentional plan of Satan, to defeat the purpose that God has in place for humanity. Eve's mind was unguarded and worse, the devil also knew that Eve's mind was unguarded and vulnerable. It was an opportunity for him to target her to use his psychological tricks in twisting the word of God. It was an opportunity to violate the command that God put in place for Adam and Eve. This couple, the first of God's creation, failed to control their issues. Instead, they chose wrong over right, a lie over truth, dishonesty over honesty, dishonor over honor and disobedience over obedience. Thanks be to God you are not a novice to the righteousness of God. Today we too are challenged with the same attacks of the devil's psychological devices. Guard your mind so that you will not fall in the same temptation.

Proverbs 4:23 states, "Keep thy heart with all diligence; for out of it are the issues of life". In 1 Peter 1:13 it says, "Wherefore gird up the loins of your mind, to be sober, and hope to the end for the grace that is to be brought unto you at the revelation of Jesus Christ".

Issues will always be a part of a human's lifestyle; we are subject to failure. Some people may cover their failures and try to discover yours, but the beauty about it is, that issues are controllable.

Our physical body is subject to disease, weakness and other crisis's, both internal and external. You may be nervously anxious about what's taking place internally, but it is no secret to your maker because he knows you inside and out. Paul wrote, "He can be touched with the feelings of our infirmities." Hebrews 4:15 reiterates "For we have not a high priest which cannot be touched with the feeling of our infirmities; but was in all points tempted like as we are, yet without sin". In 2 Corinthians 4:16 it says, "For which cause we faint not; but though our outward man perish, yet the inward man is renewed day by day". Although the non-physical body is invisible, it is more vulnerable than the physical body; so while we care for the outward, your maker takes care of the inward. Him alone can see what human eyes cannot see and touch where human hands cannot touch. So, when issues occur inwardly, God already knows about it. You may use these words "Oh my God, what's happening?' or "What is really going on with me?" So, we connect to him, importing and exporting, which is the source of communication when we pray; so, we ask God to take control and ask for his direction. He may direct you to that health care provider and will guide them to do the job he requires to be done on you. Of course, you consult God first to correct the problem, or he will correct it by himself. He is in control and he knows what's best for you.

Going to the health care provider does not mean that you don't believe in your creator. Of course not! You believe that God can do the job, so you consult God first. Sometimes, even before you get to the health care provider, God corrects the problem. He will have even health care providers confused when they cannot find the problem. When faith increases you will be persuaded that God will do the job.

As believers, we do research and study the Word of God that the Word may have a greater impact upon our lives, God helps our minds to be stronger and has a more positive impact on our beliefs, giving God the space to invest more and more into our lives.

You are a true believer, you know God's like and dislikes, and you have a good conscience toward godliness. Still, there are some uncontrolled issues building up in your tissues. What happened here? Satan's static power became stronger. In the beginning, he had a third of the angels working on his behalf; now his company is enlarging and he has lots of agents he can dispatch by legions, like the young man who had lived among the tomb. When that demonic spirit saw Jesus, they got scared, for at the mention of the name of Jesus, demons must flee. Satan will cause things to be problematic, his force is strong, but you got stronger power to defeat and cancel his plans (Luke 10: 19).

John Mark referred to him as the father of lies. John 8:44: "Ye are of your father the devil, and, the lust of your father ye will do. He was a murderer from the beginning, and abode not in the truth, because there is no truth in him. When he speaketh a lie, he speaketh of his own: for he is a liar and the father of it."

God gave you the power to tell Satan to get behind you, when he approaches with his pathological lies, as he did to Jesus coming off forty days of fasting. His pathological defectiveness will not enter your mind. Your mind is guarded by the Holy Ghost, who is Jesus Christ, God's Son. Jesus's blood is our coverage from all satanic attack. God told Moses to use the blood to put on the doorpost of the Israelites, that when the death angels passed by, they would see the blood and would not enter those houses. That was symbolic of the blood of Jesus Christ. So, it is today, Christ is our comprehensive coverage. Thanks be to God for the blood. A songwriter said, "The blood that gives me strength from day today shall never lose its power."

You are completely in control of the things you import and export. The devil cannot brainwash you or twist your mind with his truth because you think beyond the act of Eve.

Everything about the devil is a counterfeit. As the counterfeit dollar bill, he is the inventor of all satanic doctrines, and worshippers, the head of the Antichrist. He lets things appear like, look like, sound like, and act like, but is not right. When you know your God, you won't be deceived. Satan's foundation is built upon lies through satanic psychological plans. You may not be able to see your emotion, but you can acknowledge that your five senses are intact. You may be unable to see your emotion, but you can identify your pain. You may not be able to see your soul, but you know when you have sinned against God. You may not be able to see the spirit but may be able to discern the spirit (1 John 4:1-5 KJV).

God is a miracle worker, healer, deliverer, Savior, Balm in Gilead, way maker, salvation, master, mighty, great, powerful, the Creator. Watch out for the devil. He is a high-profile con artist and will do anything to deceive you.

The key to controlling your built-up issues, and to maintaining a consistent relationship with God is to discipline the mind from the contagious disease that will affect your spirituality. Think on good things by applying the Word of God to your life. God will supply you with wisdom to navigate and empower you. God has given you the persuasion, the authority, the right, and the power to control and put under your feet the works of the flesh; the mind will be furnished and focus on the fruits of the spirit.

Remember the devil can overhear your conversation. He's got his secret agents on the loose; he may even realize you are too powerful for him, so he uses people that are close to you to test you. Job's wife said, "curse God and die" (Job 2:9). He thought he got her twisted as he did with Eve, but Job was well-prepared, he had him under control. Job was smart and his mind was girded. Be on your double watch. The devil is a convicted criminal, a pedophile. He's on death row and his sentencing is near; he's mad, prying after souls. To the married be submissive to your husband, to the un-married be submissive to the Word of God; obey His commandments and walk in His statutes. We are called the weaker vessel as we are susceptible to voices because of the charisma. You can't be naïve. The devil targeted Eve, not Adam. I guarantee you if he had attacked Adam first, the devil would have surely been defeated. Here comes the deceiver again attacking Job and trying to challenge a God-fearing man but God guarded Job's mind.

Women of God, you are committed, you are powerful, you are called and chosen to be warriors and intercessors; a voice of connection and communication for the people. You weep like Rachel for her children and you do it for the children of God, for the church, for the city, and for the world. The devil doesn't like it, but he can't do anything about it. When you are on your knees, be guaranteed that he is very nervous for doubtless, he will lose the battle.

Women are wise to stay in the will of God. Your attacker from the beginning is a soul molester and a murderer. Somebody may not be happy because you are praying too much, fasting too much, so they complain, not knowing the will of God concerning you. A warrior prays without ceasing because they are called to watch and pray more than once or twice daily, convenient or in cases of emergency. This is a ministry from God; Paul's recommendation is that you should pray without ceasing. In 1 Thessalonians 5:17 (ESV). The woman's issues were overwhelming but through her struggles, she was committed to a restricted lifestyle. God was in total control of her holistically.

CHAPTER 9
Spiritual Bankruptcy

The woman's issue led her to a state of financial complexity. She found herself "between a rock and the hard place" so to speak; she had poor health and no money. The Scripture clearly stated that she spent what she had going to the physicians, and unfortunately, they were of no help to her because her situation got worse instead of being better.

She was in a predicament where her constant blood flowing issue made her life uncomfortable, and unpleasant. Money now became a greater issue as doctors' visits were no longer affordable. In her world view everything was just failing. It may have seemed to her that her life was falling apart; life for her was very chaotic, embarrassing, and frustrating.

Beyond all these crises there were certain values that stood out, such as: ministry, patience, and endurance, notwithstanding faith, one of the world's greatest and important legacies; "for without faith it is impossible to please God" (Hebrews 11:6).

God's power through faith was about to change her life. Her issue, more or less, was a personal/private matter. If it had been kept private, then God's purpose would not have been made manifested; cultural rituals would not have been removed. For God to use her to demonstrate his power of faith, she could no longer stay behind her closed doors as she was the chosen vessel to bring about change to a society that was already molded and set in their ways.

God used Mary, the mother of Jesus, as his choice vessel to bring forth change to a world of sin; a world that was set in its own way of unrighteousness. So God prepared this woman emotionally, psychologically, mentally, physically and spiritually. She was able to cope with all the changes that she was experiencing in her body.

We are internalized by God's will and purpose to be used by him, to bring out his project. It is indeed an awesome feeling to be chosen by your maker to display his work of art, his miracles. He could not have used just anybody, it would have to be of his choice. One with the willingness, brokenness, obedience, endurance, faithfulness, kindness, and humility of a focused and wholesome mind. These are only some of the attributes and characteristics God needs. Do not forget, we are God's representatives, having these qualities is only the preparation for the presentation.

Now the whole process begins. God melts you, liquefies you as milk poured out into a vessel; you are no more yourself. Being dead to the things around you, you become a flexible tool. John said we are in the world but not of the world (John 15:19), meaning as believers you should not be a partaker of the things which are not according to the righteousness of God, but be engaged in the things which will allow you to be progressive. You must have an attitude to approach God from a spiritual aspect; you must be physically and presently in the world but not a part of its values. (John 17:14-15 KJV).

Now that you have gone through that refining process you can now see your rough path start changing dramatically. You can forgive others who have trespassed against you, enemies are at peace, you can see the hands of God upon your life and be easily led by the Lord. Things begin to happen in your life, and you are more committed to Christ and to others. God's love begins to unfold within you as there should be no hesitation to be molded by God. Molding is the next step in the process, which brings along humility with the desire to get closer to God. "Close to thee, Close to thee, all along my pilgrim journey Savior let me walk with thee", the words of Frances Crosby. In such a disposition, being a humbled dough in the hands of the baker means that you are ready to be transformed into God's masterpiece. Your maker is molding you, you will experience some pain, but that's alright, He is only getting rid of the lumps and bubbles; the process is necessary. It is not possible for you to revert to the original liquid form; you will not be the same. The process may even seem longer than expected; your adversity is circling around you, wondering what the outcome will be. Nothing good ever comes easy, your Maker is looking for perfection and He is not giving up until He gets the best of you, to fashion you. These levels are very important and also quite interesting because your Maker is the fashion designer. Your fashion designer is fashioning you, turning you around, trimming you, and removing all the un-necessaries.

Yes, you have been through some stuff, and overcame many hurdles; you are unstoppable. Many battles have been fought and you have been victorious over, and over again. This is because, God is always in the midst of your battle and through him you conquer. The higher the level, the greater the task but don't forget you are in your maker's hand.

This woman was furnished with all the attributes that God required of her. When the woman finally encountered Jesus, she had no money. As the Scripture said, she spent all she had on her attended physicians. I truly believe if she had not gone bankrupt, she would not have gone viral, and would not have met with Jesus at the time that she did. Once everything had gone from her, she was in a critical situation, but God stepped in right on time. What a God! For this woman's miracle to be manifest, God came right on time.

Understand here, the great Creator, the mighty God, he is always on time. He was on time for Sarah at the age of ninety-nine to place baby Isaac in her arms and on time to provide the lamb for Abraham to make the sacrifice. He was on time at the Red Sea for the children of Israel to walk on dry land, Daniel in the lion's den, He was on time for Shadrach, Meshach, and Abednego. He was on time for David when approaching Goliath. He has always been on time for you. When the enemy tried to kill you, when you were in the abusive relationship, when you were lied to, when lies were told on you, when you were bankrupt, he has always been on time.

God doesn't care whether you have money, whether you are rich or poor; what God desires is your soul. God owns all things. He is the Father of all creation, "For every beast of the forest is mine, the cattle on a thousand hills are mine." He has all things but yet became poor that through his poverty we might be rich (Psalm 50:10 and 2 Corinthians 8:9).

To be rich in this life is not a sin nor is it a crime; however, your riches should not control you, especially to the point where a wedge has been driven between you and your God. You should feel comfortable in your mind worshiping your Creator and be of some assistance to others in a time of need. The rich young ruler didn't have a problem in loving his neighbors but had a problem in giving up all to follow Jesus (Mark 10:17-27).

Financial challenges vary, each have their own experiences. Some manage their spending by budgeting, while some are irresponsible spenders, always spending beyond his or her means. Irresponsible spenders spend when they are happy, sad, or mad and when all is spent, the credit cards become easy access to more funds. This only furthers debt; a frugal spender not only seeks for the cheapest items but is smart in the money choices they make. Another category on the spectrum of money management is the miser who holds on to their wealth. They spend as little as possible, while the less fortunate have little or none to spend. Proverbs 30: (NLT) says "For if I grow rich, I may deny you and say, 'Who is the Lord?' And if I am too poor, I may steal and thus insult God's holy name". Whether you have money or not, money is always an issue. When there is not enough the mind gets worried, stressed, confused, gets less sleep, the physical become overworked and the non-physical gets emotionally overwhelmed. Believe it or not the rich may experience the same issues or even worst; there are restless and sleepless nights, always seeking ways for investment and can never have enough revenue coming. Bad money management eventually leads towards bankruptcy and this can be very chaotic.

No one wants to experience bankruptcy, no one wants to live life's complexities, so you govern your mind and control your spending. Limit your craving because when craving supersedes spending you are heading for bankruptcy. Pay no attention to the credit cards which is a temptation to the mind. The mind is always telling you a credit card is a must. Over indulgence with credit cards as well as poor money management also leads to incurring bad credit. However, bad credit can be repaired, although you may face some consequences for your defaults. This crisis can be very challenging, as you may experience setbacks, emotional pain, or self-contempt. However, these issues are curable, it is only a matter of time.

As a holistic body, we also experience spiritual bankruptcy. This is a type of disease that affects the body, soul, and spirit. This disease is a poison to the mind. As a matter of fact, your physical body is subject to what effects your mind because the body is dead without the mind, soul, and spirit living in it; this includes the tissues.

As believers, we must pay attention to the things we have allowed to become lodged in the mind as that will affect the spiritual demands. To quote Ephesians 6:10-12 (KJV): "Finally, my brethren, be strong in the Lord, and in the power of his might. Put on the whole armor of God, that ye may be able to stand against the wiles of the devil. For we wrestle not against flesh and blood, but against principles, against powers, against the rulers of the darkness of this world, against spiritual wickedness in high places".

It is pointless fighting against the physical body, because the physical body is harmless. So then, because you are unable to see the spiritual wickedness in high places with your physical eyes, but only through the spirit, you must pray in the spirit for God to bring down the high places, pull down the strongholds, and bring peace and deliverance to the mind. Never judge a person when they begin to act or conduct his/herself inadequately, but rather pray for them. They may be being led by six thousand spirits, like the man among the tomb.

You are a conqueror who is not up for a spiritual defeat. The disease of spiritual bankruptcy shall not lodge in your mind because you refused to accept things that are not of God. The mind is accountable for the nonphysical body, it is storage, so therefore, accept good thoughts and reject the bad thoughts at will. Paul made mention of this in I Philippians 4:8 (KJV), "Finally, brethren, whatsoever things are true, whatsoever things are honest, whatsoever things are just, whatsoever things are pure, whatsoever things are lovely, whatsoever things are of good report; if there be any virtue, and if there be any praise, think on these things".

Depositing these characteristics into your account will make the mind happy. Like the investor, the more that is deposited into the savings account, the happier it makes them. You need these characteristics to boost credibility, to get you into the mindset that allows you to access and to withdraw from your spiritual account in time of need. Your account report will be in good standing with a positive balance. Your account is you, your credibility, your honesty, your self-reliance, and integrity. If you were to deposit lies, craftiness, dishonesty, unjust, impurity and hatred into your account, it will only cause you failure. An account that has no interest, no hope, no balance, or a negative balance gives you limitations and a lifestyle filled with selfishness and defaults. However, there is something amazing about God's grace that works effectively from the inside out. In spite of your many defaults and failures, God consolidates all debts and makes your life so much stronger. God paid off that huge debt with a single one-time lump sum debt payment. He settled the account. Avoid mistakes, avoid un-confessed sins, avoid temptation, lusting and the sins that lead you to spiritual bankruptcy.

Spiritual bankruptcy is a spiritual set-back. It is an opportunity to withdraw from righteousness and move further from God. It depletes your interaction and quality time spent with God in worship, prayer and fasting. It makes you more selfish and un-willing, withdrawn from taking active part in the work of the Lord, and causes you to want more from God while giving him less. It is like you want to withdraw from your account more than what you have in the account. Whatever service you give to God, it is your accomplishment for your tomorrow; your work will speak for you. God is the manager for your personal bank account, it is a fixed deposit with your name on it; he alone has the access to your account and it cannot be tampered with nor can thief break in and steal from it. Matthew 6:20 (KJV) "But lay up for yourselves treasures in heaven, where neither moth nor rust doth corrupt, and where thieves do not break through nor steal". Spiritual bankruptcy gives a bad outlook and leaves a bad impression. It sends out messages to various businesses that your name has been "red flagged" and every creditor has turned you down; it is "cash or no deal" and each time you walk away discredited.

The woman found herself in a discreditable situation. God saw her issues, knew her pain, although she may have come in a camouflaged disposition with fear and trembling. Jesus knew she was there. Jesus moves with great compassion He said, "Daughter, go in peace they faith has made thee whole" (Luke 8:48).

Some of my flash backs just humbled me. When I remembered of some of the issues my tissues had experienced I was emotionally drained, psychologically depressed, physically depleted, but spiritually embraced and motivated to move forward. I was not able to read my bible, but thanks be to God I was able to pray and sing songs making melody in my heart unto God. My physical body was restricted because of my issues, I couldn't have left the room unless for medical purposes, as in x-rays and other tests. I felt as if bankruptcy was coming my way because I had lost my income from both jobs. I was badly set up by the adversary and his desire was for me to go bankrupt, but God stepped into my circumstances and said "I will not have you depleted or depress by any means I will take care of you, for the cattle on a thousand hills are mine." I was awarded a nil compensation for injuries. My husband then, was the only bread winner at the time. We had challenging times as a family, but I braced myself with Gods holy faith to dismiss against spiritual bankruptcy against my life.

Spiritual bankruptcy is a limitation that bars you from being active in God's vineyard and to do the task which was given to you. The five foolish virgins were spiritually bankrupt, they tried to borrow oil from the five wise virgins but were unsuccessful, and they were in a precarious situation. God provides you strategies, and resources that will protect you from getting into defaults. Defaults only bring failure and embarrassment. You need to give yourself a routine checkup, making sure your growth is progressing.

God wants your account to be in good standing. He is your investor and wants to invest in you. Sometimes you may wonder how you found yourself in this disposition, but do not allow negativities to remain in the mind. God can repair that mind and put good thoughts and fresh courage to demonstrate his power in you. You shall not go bankrupt. You refuse to invest in the flesh, and you already know that the works of the flesh lead to spiritual bankruptcy. You are smarter than that. For the flesh can only manifest itself in the flesh because flesh equals flesh. Galatians 5:19-21 says: "Now the works of the flesh are manifest, which are these; Adultery, fornication, uncleanness, lasciviousness, idolatry, witchcraft, hatred, variance, emulations, wrath, strife, seditions, heresies, Envyings, murders, drunkenness, revellings, and such like: of the which I told you before, as I have also told you in time past, that they which do such things shall not inherit the kingdom of God".

This strange disease will affect you holistically, stop your spiritual growth, leave you in despair, anger, range, hostility, and with mistrust. You can refuse to accept these diseases and declare it will not become a part of your lifestyle. Your mind belongs to God; let him have your mind.

Although this woman was quarantined, I do believe she had an internalized relationship with her Creator. God promised that he will not leave us nor forsake us in our time of need, and so did he with the Woman. God is a spirit; spirit to spirit works miracles, as faith to faith moves mountains. When it was time for deliverance, fear could not hold her back. I do believe money was no more her concern because when Jesus healed her, he covered all; she was delivered from all her issues. Do not feel restricted by your circumstances like the man by the pool for thirty-eight years, impotent and immobile, waiting for the water to be troubled, and waiting for some assistant. When God delivered you, he turned things around, from bankruptcy to luxury, from weakness to strength, immobility to mobility. God is real, this world is real, heaven is real, Satan is real, and hell is real, so keep your account in good standing, keep your focus. God promised to keep us in perfect peace if our mind stays on him.

CHAPTER 10

Faith Prevails Issues in the Tissues

The expression and demonstration of the power of faith behind the supernatural power of Jesus Christ brought healing deliverance and victory to the issues in my tissues. This profound incredible life story brought many restrictions and barriers which was only a set-up for my defeat, but the God of purpose showed up on time I then realized my years of set back was only to humbled me. One of the most phenomenal thing about my issues is that I adhered to my faith by any means would I complain but ask God to mole my faith in his. I then knew I had to endure to achieve my triumphant victory. You may have gone though some horrific moments that have created painful memories, whether it be by sickness, fear, shock, abuse, and the list go on. Due to the struggle with these issues, it may seem harder to let go of them. Every time you may have tried to let go, it comes back to your mind with a vengeance, unless you release your mind of the ongoing issues it will only bring more hurt, hate, bitterness, and anger. Releasing the issues from your mind will allow you to receive enhancement, restoration, forgiveness, and peace of mind.

It was the prayer of faith you prayed when you he showed up for you, when you were sick and couldn't get well, when the doctor's report came back negative, when you were homeless with nowhere to live and no food to eat and he showed up right on time. This too was the power of faith. It is because when you prayed, you believed that God would show up and he really did. God wants you to know he hears, answers your prayer and that he cares for you. Its only a matter of time before you will realize that faith has prevailed. Intense issues always bring a closer relationship with you and your God. It makes room for deep fellowship and great communication, and allows you to walk hand in hand with Jesus while feeling that deep, settled peace of God in an overflowing mood. When you develop that internalized communication with God, there is a built-up relationship with you and God; a deep overflowing joy that can never cease.

Our physical body will go through sickness, aches, and pain for in this body we do groan. However, when the non-physical body cries out to God, the Creator who can be touched with the feelings of the infirmed body will come through. As I've mentioned previously, when faith meets faith, mighty works are done. When spirit meets spirit, miracles take place. So therefore, it is faith that works. Jesus said to me in the vision "I looked beyond your faults and saw your needs" instantaneously faith arose I knew from that moment that I was healed.

Never think the worst, even when life seems hopeless as you struggle to survive. God will get you right back on track and prove to you that you are chosen for his demonstration. Struggle doesn't last long; it is only an experience for the next level. There is a story beyond your struggles and there is laughter beyond your tears. God has brought you this far by faith and you know he will take you to the end. Issues, struggle, and all sort of problems were on planet Earth before we got here, and sure enough, we shall also leave it here. We abuse ourselves a times and weaken our emotion over petty matters. In the end, we develop self inflected wounds; wounds which could have been avoided. If we had only release them, they would not have plagued the mind which some times leads to a stagnant state. Release your mind, even if it hurts. Your Creator is able to take care of the unthinkable and the impossible. He has done it for me.

God was aware of what would have taken place in my life, my situation wasn't new to him but he places his faith in me so that his miracle could have been made manifested in me. God knew my identity, I was not chosen mistakenly, He is my Creator and He knew me before I was made substance in my mother's womb. Psalm 139: 15 (NKJV) says, "my frame was not hidden from you when I was made secret, and skillfully wrought in the lowest part of the earth." I was that faithless and imperfect vessel, by which he made faithful and perfect; vulnerable, but valuable for God's task.

Doctors sometimes use animals or human bodies to do their experiments for research to make discoveries. God used his created human beings to demonstrate his miraculous power. You are never to be a victim of your circumstances but rather victorious. When God is finished with you, he takes you viral and makes you known. His perfect will has been established in you as God prepared you holistically: body, soul, and spirit.

I am a very private person and would had like to keep my issues private and confidential, imagine: being diagnosed with cancer, broken leg and a heart attack all simultaneously but here God used me for his demonstration to allow faith to prevail, I had to be unveiled to reveal God's plan. God used me as his chosen vessel, as he used the woman with her issues of blood. God used the woman as a chosen vessel to bring change to society that was so molded to a culture that was very set in their ways. God used Mary, the mother of our Lord Jesus Christ, as a chosen vessel to bring change to a world of sin, to a world that was also set in its own ways of unrighteousness Luke 1:30-31 says, "And the angel said unto her, fear not, for thou has found favor with God. And behold, thou shall conceive in thy womb and bring forth a son, and shall call his name Jesus. I believe God had prepared this woman holistically to accept all the necessary changes and challenges she would have had to experience in her tissues. Gods only desire was for faith to prevail over cultural ritual.

Circumstances can appear as high walls. Surrounded by mountain, trouble on each side and all you see before your eyes is dead end, no exit. It is your Red Sea experience. I could not have run from my circumstances, but endured through it. If God takes you to it he will lead you through it. Ernest W. Blandy wrote, "I'll go with him through the waters, I'll go with him through the waters, I'll go with him…with him all the way."

Lying there in the ICU, I reached out by faith and touched Jesus with an expectation, my faith has prevailed victory over circumstance.

You need faith to prevail when circumstances intensify. When pain gets extremely severe, when the storms wont stop ranging, when the battle gets intense, when the Giants get in the way, when all hell breaks loose, when you are place in the lion's den, when you are put in the fiery furnace, when you have been lied to, when you are ignored, when you are singled out, when you are denounced or demoted, life seems unbalanced and peace cannot be found. When the bills cannot be paid because the account is empty, how do you see God here? When life seems to be so pinned down by your circumstances, how do you see God here?

I saw God in my spirit world view, then I reached out by faith. Note the physical cannot move unless the spirit moves it. When you see Jesus, reach out to him by faith through the non-physical body, not by the physical body, your whole world will change. Faith prevailed as God broke down the wall of segregation for the woman with her issue of blood to bring equality and freedom to her world that was subjected to fear. Jesus broke down the middle wall of partition for the Gentiles by his shed blood on the cross, giving us free access and right to the throne of grace. God's mercies have been extended to us, that we might have life more abundantly. Peter only understands the mystical deliverance of the Gentiles barrier when Jesus unfolded it to him in a vision at Joppa (Acts 10:11-16).

Let faith be your weapon against fear. Esther used faith as her weapon against fear when she said in, Esther 4:16 (KJV) "If I perish, I perish". Esther decided that she would not be defeated by threats to sit with King Ahasuerus and defend her faith. Faith must prevail over your issues to be victorious.

The woman said, "If I only touch the hem of his garment, I shall be made whole." She had expectation, determination, and perseverance; her faith prevailed.

There is no need to stand in jeopardy, or to sit by the pool waiting. It is time for you to take authority, accept your faith miracle, your faith victory, your faith deliverance, and your healing Psalm 121: 1-8 this is your faith season. God is saying "I know you have gone through many things and are still going through, but this is your season your night will soon be past." God's night is not on your schedule, God's night could be the next second, the next minute, the next hour, may be the next day or year. Who knows God's hour? "and a thousand years as one day" (2 Peter 3:8). Issues will come but issues must go when faith prevails.

Thanks be to God who has given victory through the power of faith. Today persons who have done the heart surgery still have issues and are under the care of doctors. To this day I have received calls from person I never knew but who have known of my issues having regrets for doing heart surgery. As of today, they are physically restricted. I still believe there is hope, it is only a matter of time for faith to prevail. God is always willing to work with whatever faith you have, even the mustard seed faith. It is a fact that when God heals or delivers you, you are completely healed or delivered -just like the woman with the issue of blood she was completely dried up. Let faith prevail ove issues.

You might have been targeted, set-up and set-back, but he delivered you from all your attackers and allowed angles to encamp around you. You have conquered your fears. You have learned how to suffer and how to be courageous, to be grateful, to be thankful, patient, and how to depend on God. He didn't deliver you because you are beautiful, special or righteous, but because of his divine favor. You can be an envelope for others. You can live a life of legacy to touch the lives of others. God has given you the tools along with strategies and resources. You are smart and you know how to super-sede allow faith to prevail over issues in the tissues.

- This is your season, faith has triumphed
- Tissues have been healed
- Tissues have been restored
- The mind is at peace
- Psychological statics have been frozen
- Your spirit has been set free
- Your soul is satisfied
- Your holistic self has been restored
- Cultural rituals have been abolished

- Fears have been subsided
- Your true identity has been discovered
- You are God's daughter
- You are free from psychological prison
- You are free from limitation
- You are free from isolation
- You are bound from satanic works or plans
- You stand in the power of faith
- The will of almighty God is over your life
- The purpose of God has manifested in you
- You are in God's will
- You are destined for greatness
- God used you to demonstrate his power
- He manifested his gift of faith in you
- He lives in you and you in him
- Your physical body is earthy
- Your non-physical soul and spirit are heavenly
- You are highly favored.
- You will not succumb to the issues in your tissues
- You shall live and not die
- Faith has prevailed over all issues in the tissues
- The walls have been broken down
- Live.

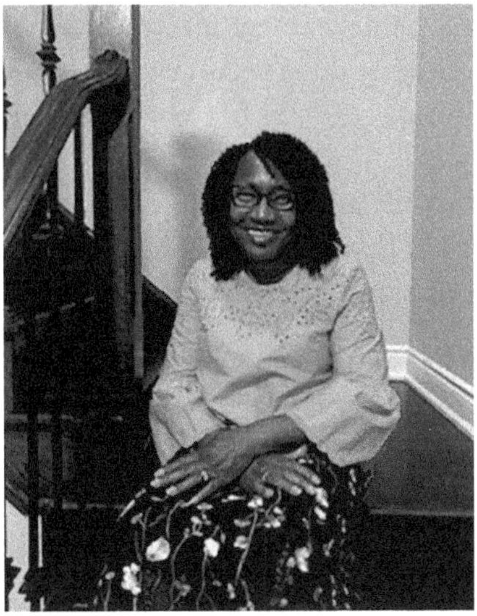

ABOUT THE AUTHOR

Missionary Millicent Plummer Robinson served as the assistant women's director of the Gracious Women of God Ministry for a period of three years, then moved into the role of director of said ministry for an additional three years at the Rest Tabernacle Church of Jesus Christ in Toronto, Ontario, Canada, under the leadership of Bishop E. R. Thomas.

Millicent is also the author of five other books: *The Journey's of Faith, Hope and Trust; Behind the Veil of the Temple; I am Who I am; Whimpy the Caterpillar; and God's Creation.*

CPSIA information can be obtained
at www.ICGtesting.com
Printed in the USA
BVHW071635181220
595733BV00002B/109

9 781098 034795